YOUNG GOL..........

PETER SMITH & BEVERLY LEWIS

GUINNESS PUBLISHING

Young Golfer

Published in Great Britain by Guinness Publishing Ltd, 33 London Road, Enfield, Middlesex.

Designed by MasterClass Publishing Ltd, Birmingham. Tel: 021-471 4964.
Typesetting & reproduction by Meridian Media Services, Meridian House, Bakewell Road, Orton Southgate, Peterborough, Cambs PE2 0XU.
Photographs by Ken Lewis, Peter Smith, Photosport International.
Illustrations © Ken Lewis 1992.
Printed and bound in Great Britain by The Bath Press.

"Guinness" is a registered trademark of Guinness Publishing Ltd.

A catalogue record for this book is available from the British Library.

ISBN 0-85112-533-6

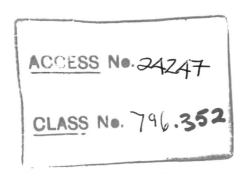

Acknowledgements

We wish to thank the following for their very kind assistance:

Richard Bradford

Lee Bowyer

Simon Kuker

Gareth Lamb

Louise Fletcher

Langdon Hills Golf Club

Newcastle-under-Lyme Golf Club

John Reay Golf Shops

Young Golfer

A young Nick Faldo – it's a long hard climb to the top.

Contents

page

Introduction	7
In the Beginning	9
A background to golf – Scoring.	
Equipment	12
Clothes	14
Getting to Grips	15
The basic grip – Grip pressure – Major faults.	
A Quality Address	20
Getting ready to swing the club – Targetting – Fault finder.	
The Golf Swing	28
Backswing – Downswing – The plane – Fault finder.	
Power v Accuracy	46
Which is more important?	
Pro Quote	49
Ronan Rafferty on equipment.	
On the Tee	50
Beginning the round – Major faults.	
Pro Quote	57
Seve Ballesteros on practising.	
On the Fairway	58
Approaching Perfection	62
Approach shots – The short irons – Chipping – Pitching – Round the green strategy.	
Pro Quote	67
Brett Ogle on starting young.	
Hazards	68
Bunkers; The splash shot – Long bunker shots – Plugged lie – Bunker practice – Bunker etiquette.	
Having a Rough Time	76
Tips on getting out of trouble.	

page

On the Green	82
Putting; Reverse overlap grip – Marking the ball – Pitch mark repair – Practice.	
The Rules of Golf	92
On the tee – Obstructions and impediments – Out of Bounds – Ground under repair – Water Hazards – Casual water – Divots and animal scrapings – On the green – Lost ball – Unplayable ball.	
Pro Quote	103
Practical tips from Steve Richardson.	
Etiquette	104
Course Strategy	108
On the green – Weather conditions – How to play in wind and rain – Sloping lies – Sidehill lies – Hitting the ball high – Hitting the ball low.	
Practice Makes Perfect	122
Advice on practice.	
Look and Learn	126
Learn by watching the professionals.	
And Finally	142
Advice on playing and competing – The Golf Foundation – Daily Telegraph Junior Golfer of the Year – The Esso Golf Classic.	
Pro Quote	147
Sandy Lyle on practising.	
How to become a Golf Professional	148
Making a career out of golf.	
Glossary	156
Some Useful Addresses	158
Index	159

CHURCHILL SCHOOL

"Every champion starts somewhere." Greg Norman, Open Champion 1986.

Introduction

Golf is one of the most exciting and challenging games in the world, as well as one of the most popular. It is, like most games, best taken up at an early age when the learning process is so much easier.

Many of today's top players began playing golf when they were very young – Nick Faldo and Seve Ballesteros among them. Both became interested in golf for different reasons; Ballesteros began his golf "career" caddying whilst still a young boy in northern Spain; Faldo became interested whilst watching Jack Nicklaus on television – little did he realise that one day he would be playing alongside his boyhood idol.

The growth of television coverage of golf tournaments has given many young people the opportunity to watch and study the great golfers of today, yet it is so much better, having watched them, to get out there and play yourself.

Some schools include golf in their sporting curriculum; many parents play and introduce their children to the game; for others, self-motivation will take them to the nearest golf club for some lessons during summer holidays. Others will just go to the driving range and hit golf balls, perhaps with a borrowed club or two.

Whatever the route into golf you take, it is essential that you have some lessons from a qualified golf professional. Learning from the very beginning how to grip the club, how to stand and how to swing will pay dividends immediately, putting you firmly on the road to becoming a good golfer.

This book, using lessons from professional golfers, will help you to understand the background to playing golf. Using it in conjunction with les-

You're never too young to take up golf!

Introduction

sons from your golf professional and plenty of self-dedication might put you on the road to a top golfing career – it will certainly help you to enjoy your game to the full.

An important note here to parents. Golf may well have given you a great deal of pleasure, as well as countless frustrations! By ensuring your son or daughter receives proper, qualified, professional instruction, you can give them a head start into the world of golf. Some instruction classes are free of charge, but it is well worth investing in a half-dozen lessons, perhaps as a birthday or Christmas present, to really get the ball rolling, or rather, flying!

Even top professionals have lessons! The familiar figure of Masters Champion Ian Woosnam working hard on the practice ground, watched by coach Bob Torrance.

In The Beginning

Golf has been played in the form we know it today for at least 500 years, having started in Scotland around 1400 on the piece of land that is still used today as the Old Course, St Andrews. It evolved from earlier games played in Holland and France and which were brought across by traders.

Whatever the true origin of golf, lost forever in the depths of time, the Scots popularised the game and spread it worldwide. The greatest golfers of the 19th century, when its popularity increased dramatically, were all Scots, including Old Tom Morris and his son Young Tom Morris, Willie Park, James Braid and others. A host of Scots golfers migrated to America around 1900 to firmly establish the game there.

The first British Open was held in 1860 at Prestwick, played over a course which had only twelve holes; at that time there was no agreed number of holes a course should have – some had 22. Gradually, with the available land, eighteen holes became the norm and has remained so.

The early courses were all on the coast, on the sandy areas of dune or other semi-permanent land which links the sea and the town – hence the term "links" to describe such a course. Sheep used to graze on this land, keeping vegetation low and scrubby, with few trees and thin grass on which the ball runs considerable distances.

Where the grass had been eaten away, sandy areas came up through the thin soil, giving us bunkers, or

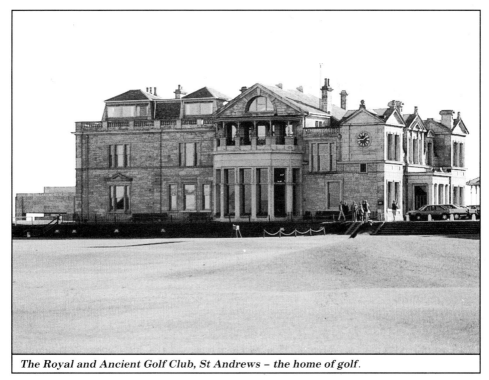

The Royal and Ancient Golf Club, St Andrews – the home of golf.

9

In The Beginning

sand traps as they are called in America. They became a feature of links courses and are now built into virtually every golf course, whether a links or an inland course.

Courses today comprise eighteen holes (though there are some nine-hole courses) and most of them have a "par" of around 72. The "par" is the number of strokes it should take a good player to complete the course and is calculated according to the length of each hole.

On most courses there are four par-3 holes, measuring up to 245 yards, ten par-4 holes, measuring between 276 and 475 yards; and four par-5s, from 476 yards and longer. There are one or two par-6 holes in Hawaii and a par-7 in Australia, but anything above about 550 yards is rare.

You start each hole from the tee. The men's competition tees are usually marked with white boxes, the non competition tees are yellow, the ladies tees are red, and juniors are blue. Not all courses have junior tees so, depending on your ability, you would play from the ladies' or men's yellow tees to start with.

The mown area of grass between the tee and green is called the fairway, the uncut areas are rough. The hole is situated on the green, which has fine manicured grass on it.

To make golf more interesting a handicap system was devised in 1925 whereby a golfer's ability was taken

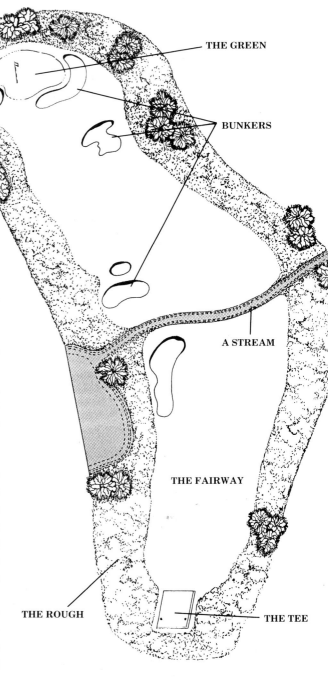

THE GREEN

BUNKERS

A STREAM

THE FAIRWAY

THE ROUGH

THE TEE

A typical par-4 hole showing some of the features you are likely to encounter.

Scoring

into account in adding up his or her score. With the average par of a golf course being 72 those golfers who regularly scored 80 were given a "handicap" of eight. Those regularly scoring 90 were given a handicap of eighteen and so on. Thus, if a player with a handicap of five was playing one with a handicap of twenty, the two would be evenly matched, the better player having to score 77 to achieve a "net par" score, the player with a handicap of twenty needing to score 92 to achieve the same result.

Handicaps are still used today to ensure a degree of equality in any game between players whose abilities may vary considerably. Handicaps are decided by the results of several rounds played once you have joined a golf club.

The holes on a golf course, too, use a form of "handicapping"; each hole is given a "stroke index" denoting its degree of difficulty, stroke index one being the hardest, stroke index (S.I.) 18 the easiest.

A "par" is scored when the hole is completed in the number of strokes shown on the scorecard, three, four or five. One over (eg, a five on a par-4) is known as a bogey – named after the unliked "bogey-man" of a children's rhyme of the last century. Two shots over is a double bogey and so on.

One under par (eg. a three on a par-4) is a "birdie"; two under is an "eagle"; three under (very rare but it would be a two on a par-5 or a hole-in-one on a par-4) is an albatross.

A hole-in-one is scored when the tee-shot goes straight into the hole. Despite odds of 43,000 to 1 against, some players are extremely lucky or clever in holing in one. The world's leader is believed to be Norman Manley, an amateur player from Long Beach, California, who has achieved no less than 47 holes-in-one including two in succession, both par-4s, in September 1964 when he aced the 7th (330 yards) and 8th (290 yards) in a record beating round of 61 – ten under par!

Time:			Competition :					Date :			Result :	

HILVERSUMSCHE GOLF CLUB

Player: ▲   Handicap :   Strokes :

LOCAL RULES

Marker	Hole	meters Men	meters Ladies	Par	Stroke	Player's result	Marker	Hole	meters Men	meters Ladies	Par	Stroke	Player's result
	1	456	440	5	15			10	145	126	3	16	
	2	314	302	4	11			11	385	335	4	4	
	3	390	325	4	5			12	322	312	4	8	
	4	383	318	4	3			13	444	384	5	12	
	5	204	164	3	13			14	116	100	3	18	
	6	416	366	4	1			15	415	335	4	2	
	7	446	429	5	7			16	383	308	4	6	
	8	130	123	3	17			17	360	303	4	14	
	9	339	299	4	9			18	452	420	5	10	
	Out	3078	2766	36				In	3022	2623	36		
								Out	3078	2766	36		
								Tot.	6100	5389	72		

Signatures :   SSS 72

Marker :

Player :

Handicap

Nett

1. Out of bounds is marked by white paint on poles.

2. Ground under repair is marked with blue paint on poles or by signs indicating the area. A ball laying on 'ground under repair' **MUST** be lifted and dropped or placed in accordance with the rules.

3. Sprinkler heads and controlboxes are considered immovable obstructions.

4. Out of Bounds (Rule 29-1 and Def. 21) At the 10th hole, beyond the line of white stakes along the edge of the 10th 'fairway' and short of the line joining the last stake to the single white stake on the other side of the driving range.

A typical scorecard showing the length of each hole, its par and its stroke index.

Equipment

Buying the right equipment is very important. A good golf professional will match clubs to suit your game and build and it is important to make sure that the lie of the clubs (see page 13), the grip size, the length and weight are correct. You will undoubtedly grow out of your first set of clubs, so be sure to seek professional advice whenever you change them. Remember, the most expensive clubs will not make you a good golfer, but the correct clubs for your height and strength will enable you to become one.

The player up to 12 or 13 must guard against using clubs that are too heavy and long for them. Ideally they should have a junior half set, which has 5, 7, 9 irons, a sand wedge, 5-wood, and putter, or 4, 6, 8, wedge, 5-wood and putter. You can, of course, buy another wood, a 3-wood which would help you gain more distance from the tee, but for beginners the 5-wood is perfectly acceptable for tee shots and from the fairway.

It is quite possible that even in a junior set the clubs might be too long for some players, in which case grip the club a little way down the shaft until you have grown enough to be able to grip comfortably at the end of the club.

Once you have outgrown a junior set, you may find that ladies' clubs are quite suitable; they are lighter and shorter than men's and have a whippier shaft. The grip is also thinner, which for small hands is ideal. The correct grip thickness will allow your left hand fingers to almost touch the base of the thumb when gripped.

Once you get stronger and taller,

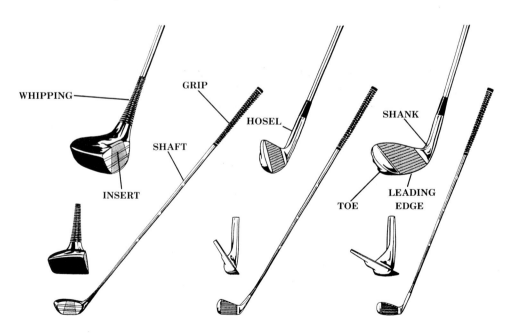

Various golf clubs – the Driver (left), a 5-iron (centre). The Driver has very little loft; the pitching wedge is very lofted to get the ball up in the air.

Equipment

you will need to change the clubs, but still beware clubs that are too heavy. Ask your professional's advice, and he will check the five important aspects:

● Grip thickness
● Flex of the shaft
● Length of shaft
● Weight of the club
● Lie of the club

A full set of golf clubs, maximum of fourteen, normally comprises three woods (which can be metal woods) numbered 1, 3, and 5 (though you can buy 4-woods and 7-woods); the irons range from 1 to 9 and then there are pitching wedges and sand wedges.

You also need a putter, which comes in many shapes and sizes. Be sure that the shaft is not too long that it sticks into your stomach. Your professional will advise you, and will cut down the shaft if need be.

Look after your clubs, every so often scrubbing the grips in warm soapy water to remove the dirt and grease, and keep the grooves on the irons free from mud. After your game,

remove the head covers from wooden clubs to allow them to dry if they are wet.

The golf bag itself is an important part of the equipment and should be large and strong enough to carry and protect your clubs, yet not so large that it is difficult to carry or transport around. For graphite clubs your bag should be specially adapted to offer more protection to the shafts, or you should buy the special graphite head covers for woods and irons.

Head covers are essential for all woods, whether wood or metal, and a putter head cover is also useful. Covers for irons are available but are not always essential as the iron heads are, themselves, strong enough to withstand normal wear and tear, provided they are looked after.

Most bags come complete with a rain cover which will keep the clubs dry if you are playing in the rain. It will also protect your clubs away from the golf course. If you are travelling by air or train with your clubs a travel bag is also a very worthwhile investment.

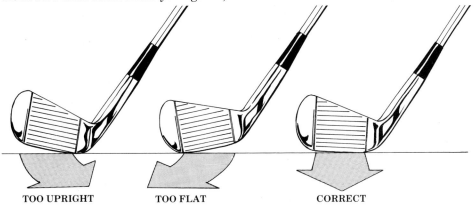

TOO UPRIGHT   TOO FLAT   CORRECT

Lie of a club. If the lie is too upright (left) the heel of the club catches the ground first, often causing a hook. Too flat (centre) does the opposite, causing a slice. A well-fitted club (right) is as essential as it would be for a pair of shoes.

Clothes

The clothes you wear on the golf course should be comfortable above all else, though "dress codes" at most courses prohibit football shorts; jeans; collarless, vest type, football or slogan T-shirts and other items which would not be in keeping with the image of golf. Tailored shorts are normally allowed, particularly for young golfers and for ladies, but glaring colours and vivid patterns are not, generally, welcomed.

In cooler weather a sweater is essential, and waterproofs are also vital if you are playing in the rain.

A golf glove, worn on the left hand for those playing right handed, helps to give better grip in that hand, but it is not essential. Those with small hands may have difficulty getting a glove to fit – it should be quite tight – and an ill-fitting glove is of no use, as it might allow the club to turn in the hands when being swung. Whilst most professionals use gloves they often take them off for putting and short shots. The long-hitting American golfer Freddie Couples does not use a glove at all.

Golf shoes come in two basic types – rubber soled for summer when fairways are hard, and spikes, for use at all other times. Naturally, spikes give a better grip year round and all tournament professionals choose them whatever the weather. You can also buy waterproof shoes for the winter, though, being rubber rather than leather, they are less comfortable in the summer.

Shoes must really be well looked after and cleaned regularly, using some leather polish rather than just the liquid whitener used on many canvas and other sports shoes.

A well dressed young golfer.

Getting To Grips

As golf is played by swinging a club it is fairly obvious that the way the club is held is of prime importance.

To play good golf the ball must be hit reasonably straight; to achieve this the club must be square to the ball-to-target line at the point of impact. If the club face is pointing left, called closed, the ball will go left – if pointing right, called open, the ball will go right.

Consistently getting the club face back into the correct position, demands that the club be gripped correctly. The most widely used grip is the overlapping, or Vardon grip, named after the great Jersey professional who won the British Open a record six times between 1896 and 1914. He did not actually invent the grip, it having been in use for many years before he was born. What he did was to popularise it by his success and consistency.

The way to grip the club correctly is as follows: With the club face square to the target, first place the club in your left hand with the grip lying across the middle joint of your first finger. The butt end of the grip is then positioned under the heel of the hand, level with the base of the thumb when the hand is laid open. The fingers then close round the grip with the thumb positioned slightly to right of centre on the shaft.

As you look down, you should see two to two-and-a-half knuckles on your left hand. The back of the hand should be pointing virtually towards the target.

Now for the right hand. The little finger of the right hand is placed over the valley formed by the first and second fingers of the left hand as they grip the club. The remaining fingers are then placed on the grip, the first finger being slightly "triggered", leaving a small gap between the middle finger and the forefinger. The fleshy pad under the thumb of the right hand is placed over the left thumb as the right thumb is placed slightly to the left of the centre of the shaft.

There are, though, two important alternatives if your hands are small.
1. Adopt the Vardon grip but put the

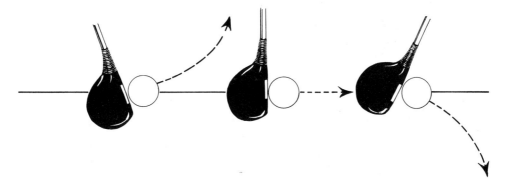

If you align the club face left, you risk hitting the ball left. If you align it to the right, you will probably hit it to the right. Aim it straight if you want to hit the ball straight.

15

right little finger on top of the left forefinger, and not between it and the middle finger.

2. Use the Baseball grip. This is where all your fingers are on the grip, rather than straining to overlap the little finger. Be sure that both hands are close together, because they must work as a unit.

There is another grip, where the little finger of the right hand and forefinger of the left interlock. Known as the interlocking grip, it has been used very successfully by Jack Nicklaus, but does weaken the control in the left hand, and is not often taught.

With the club head placed on the ground your grip should look like that in the illustration, with the "V"s formed by the thumb and first finger of each hand being parallel and pointing to a spot between the right eye and right shoulder.

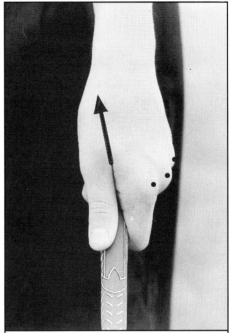
Two-and-a-half knuckles should be seen on the left hand.

First, place the club in your left hand...

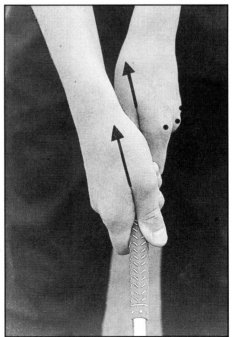
The right hand fits into position. Note the two 'V's pointing to the same spot.

Getting To Grips

Grip Pressure

It is essential you do not grip too tightly. The main pressure fingers are the last three fingers of the left hand, and middle two of the right. Pressure should only be firm enough to control the club, with the hands still feeling soft, not hard on the grip. Imagine how tightly you would hold a ball to throw it; this would be about the correct pressure for the grip.

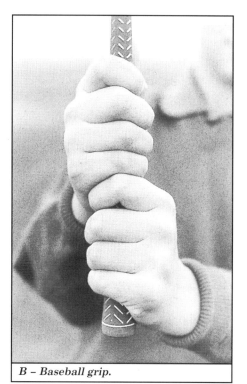

B – Baseball grip.

A – Vardon grip.

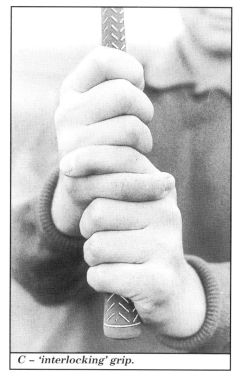

C – 'interlocking' grip.

Three main grips used.
A – the traditional Vardon grip.
B – the 'baseball' or ten-finger grip.
C – the 'interlocking' grip used
by Jack Nicklaus.

Getting To Grips

Major Faults

One of the most common faults seen in the grip is the "strong" grip, where, because the hands are turned too far to the right, they work too strongly in the swing, closing the club face at impact. This grip, where the "V"s point too far to the right, normally leads to the ball being hooked, or sent flying to the left, out of control.

A "weak" grip, where the hands are turned too far to the left, is also a major fault. From this position they cannot work actively enough in the swing, leaving the club face open at impact. This grip, where the "V"s point too far to the left, causes the ball to be sliced to the right.

The correct grip is where the hands are perfectly married, the back of the left hand pointing at the target, the "V"s pointing between the right side of the face and the right shoulder.

As you become stronger, and your hands work more actively in your swing, you may need to make minor adjustments to be able to consistently produce a square club face at impact. Remember the grip is one of the most important factors to becoming a good golfer, so practise gripping the club even on days that you don't play.

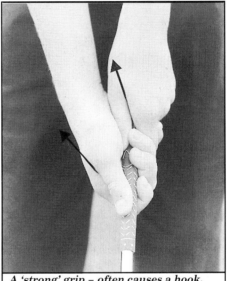

A 'strong' grip – often causes a hook.

A club gripped in the palm prevents correct wrist cocking.

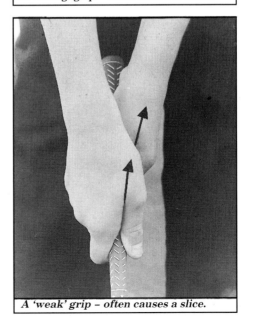

A 'weak' grip – often causes a slice.

Getting to grips

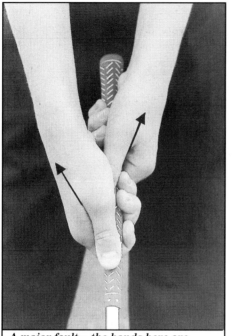

A major fault – the hands here are working against one another.

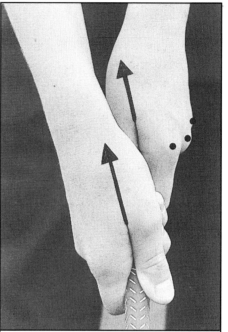

The 'V's must be pointing to a spot between the right ear and shoulder.

The correct grip is essential if you are to achieve this standard – Ian Woosnam finishes a shot in style.

A Quality Address

New Zealander Frank Nobilo at perfect address position.

A Quality Address

Once the correct grip has been ingrained in the muscle memory the next thing to understand is the way to address the ball.

It might seem such an easy thing to do but many newcomers to golf get it wrong. Your swing is almost totally predetermined by your set-up, and even the top golfers, who play almost every day, will constantly monitor their address position. Even for them, it is vital that the ball position and body alignment are just as they want them. If their posture or weight distribution is incorrect, despite their great ability, accuracy will suffer.

It is important to be relaxed at address, since any tension will inhibit you from developing a good coiling action in the backswing, which is essential if you are to achieve your maximum power at impact.

Golf professionals go through the same routine every time before hitting a shot and it is good practice to do the same, even at the driving range or on the practice area. It takes a little extra time than just standing there hitting shots pointlessly, but it ensures you get into the correct position every single time.

Having selected your club, grip it correctly, then stand behind the ball looking down the imaginary line to the target. Choose a small mark – it could be a leaf or a dry piece of grass – on the ground about two or three feet in front of the ball on that line to the target.

Next, with your feet together opposite the ball, aim the clubface squarely to an imaginary line between the ball and the intermediate target. Line the club up by having the bottom groove on the club totally square to your target.

When lowering the club to the ground, make sure that you bend forward from the hips, not the waist, creating a space in which your arms can hang freely, and swing. The photograph of Frank Nobilo illustrates this very clearly. This correct posture, where the spine remains fairly straight, but angled forward, will enable you to stand the correct distance from the ball, obviously closer with the short irons than with the longer clubs.

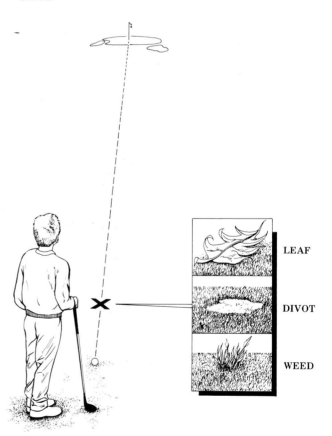

LEAF

DIVOT

WEED

Looking for intermediate target.

21

A Quality Address

Now put your feet apart, so that for your iron shots the ball is just about centrally between your feet. The width of stance will depend on your build, not too wide so that you cannot transfer your weight, but not too narrow so that you are unbalanced when you swing. For most very young golfers a stance just wider than their shoulders should be ideal. As you grow your stance will need adjusting, most players getting their stance too wide rather than too narrow.

The ball is placed centrally opposite the feet for iron shots so that the ball is struck while the club head is still descending.

When you hit a wood from the fairway, position the ball about 1 inch nearer your left foot so that you hit it when the club head is moving parallel to the ground, sweeping the ball away.

When the ball is on the tee, play the ball about 1 inch further forward than for the fairway wood, so that you hit the ball just as the club starts to swing upwards.

The width of stance increases as the clubs get longer, so that it is narrowest when playing the short irons, and widest for the driver.

Once you become stronger you may need to play the ball further forward in your stance for all shots as your leg action increases.

Your knees must be flexed, but not too bent. You should have more

Feet together opposite the ball. *Frank Nobilo again – perfectly poised.*

weight on the balls of your feet than on your heels. Check this by moving each heel in turn up and down. In this correct position you should feel as though you could jump forwards over the ball.

Again, depending on your build and flexibility, you may be able to turn better by turning each foot out slightly.

The amount of weight on each foot varies very slightly from shot to shot, but first get set up with your weight evenly distributed between your two feet. On a long shot, such as a drive, your weight should be very slightly on the back (right) foot; on a short shot, such as a pitch or bunker shot, your weight will be slightly more on the front (left) foot. For normal shots, which is how you should practise, your weight is equal on both feet.

If you look at yourself face on in a mirror, your left arm should be straight but not stiff, and should form a straight line with the shaft. This means your hands are just ahead of the ball. Your right elbow should be slightly flexed, and pointing towards your right hip.

Every golfer wants the ball to go straight, or at least to a clearly defined target. To do that, as with firing an arrow from a bow, or a gun at a video shooting range, you have to aim in the right place.

Whilst taking your address position as described above, you must make certain that you have aligned your shoulders, hips, knees and feet parallel to the target line. This may sound easy, but is seldom correct in club golfers. Practise by laying two clubs on the ground parallel to each other, one just outside the ball aimed at the target, the other across your toes. You can imagine these are railway lines,

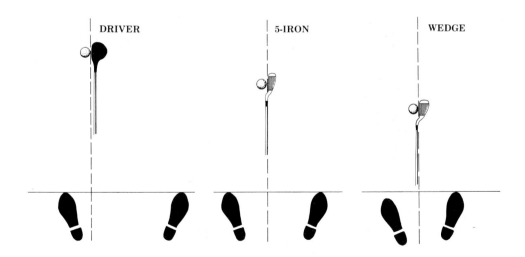

Ball-feet position. The ball is slightly further forward for the driver, gradually moving back to close to the centre for the wedge.

the ball and club head on the far one, and your feet on the nearer one.

Also, get a friend to place a club across the front of your shoulders and hips to check that they are parallel to the club on the ground.

When practising with the clubs on the ground, you can also check that you do have the club face square at address, something which sounds easy but can easily be overlooked.

The correct position of the body is called square; when the body aims too much to the left, this is called open, too much to the right is called closed.

This is the opposite to describing similar club faults, where open means aimed to the right, and closed means aimed to the left.

In winter, when bad weather may prevent you playing, practise indoors in front of a mirror. Face on you can check the ball, hand and arm position, and with the mirror to your right, you can check your posture and alignment.

Swinging the club like Faldo or Ballesteros may take years of practise, but in a matter of weeks you can look as good as them at address.

Completing the set-up: move the left foot forwards first to get the ball position correct (left); then the right foot to complete it, being perfectly balanced (right).

Targetting

When you are setting up to your target imagine you are standing on a railway line – the ball is on the far rail. Your feet, knees, hips and shoulders should all be pointing along the near rail, leaving you perfectly targeted.

Fault Finder

Most faults in a set-up can be seen easily by any observer – Tony Jacklin once said that you must look like a golfer, even if you can't hit the ball. Whilst we are all trying to hit the ball well, it is vital to get into good set-up positions and copying what top players do will certainly help.

One major fault is bending from the waist and having the legs straight.

You must bend from the hips, keeping the spine as

Fault –spine angled too much, legs too straight.

Fault – spine too erect.

straight as possible. This helps you to turn correctly.

You also need to have your knees slightly flexed, otherwise you will be too stiff and wooden. Relax and bend the knees – if you find you are then too close to the ball, move back very slightly.

"Keep your head down" is a well known golf saying, but is easily mis-interpreted. At address your head should be up, so that your chin is not on your chest, but your eyes should be looking down. If your chin is on your chest you will not be able to turn your shoulders freely. As we shall see shortly, a steady head is essential to a good swing, so keep your head up.

Fault Finder

Top: Fault – stretching too much. Get closer to the ball.

Centre: Fault – legs too straight.

Bottom: Fault – spine too rounded, head down making it difficult to swing.

Frank Nobilo at the end of a fine shot – facing the target and perfectly balanced.

The Golf Swing

So far we have looked at the ingredients that are necessary before it is possible to make a good swing. Now we come to that part where we get started on the cooking, the actual swing itself.

The swing is a totally linked set of movements around a fixed point – the large bone at the top of the spine. They all flow into one another rather than being distinct, separate actions. The club is swung in a large circle around this fixed point and the ball is struck whilst this movement is made.

Top of backswing – the shoulders and hips have turned, the club is no further than horizontal and the head is steady and over the ball. The good golfer turns on the backswing – do not sway.

Finishing – the player has turned to face the target, the right knee kicking across as the weight transfers to the left foot. Again, balance is vital.

29

The Golf Swing

One of the best ways to understand where you are trying to swing the golf club is to imagine that the ball has the hours of a clock around it.

A direct line to the target would run from 3 to 9 o'clock as you look down at the ball.

You must start with the club face square to this line and therefore facing the target.

As you swing the club back it will gradually swing inside the target line so that it travels between 3 and 4 o'clock.

In order to hit the ball straight at the target it must return along the same line so that it approaches the ball from the area between 3 and 4 o'clock. It then hits the ball whilst it is swinging towards the target at 9 o'clock, then gradually swings inside the target line again. This swing path is called in-to-in, and is evident in most good golfers' action. Providing the club face is square, the ball will travel straight towards your target.

If you hit a lot of shots that start a little left of the target then curve to the right, or shots that travel straight left, then you are swinging the club head too much from outside the target line, more in the direction of 2-8 o'clock as it approaches the ball. This swing path is called out-to-in.

Try picturing very strongly where you wish the club head to swing as it approaches the ball. If you are practising you could score a line in the grass to indicate this, or use tee pegs or another club laid down to encourage the correct swing path.

You may be one of the very few golfers who swings the club too much from inside the target line, more in the direction of 4 to 10 o'clock, as it approaches the ball. This swing path is called in-to-out, and will make you hit shots that go straight to the right, or start right then curve to the left.

Check your aim and grip, then really concentrate on that segment between 3 and 4 o'clock, and you may become your club champion, or even one of the best players in the world.

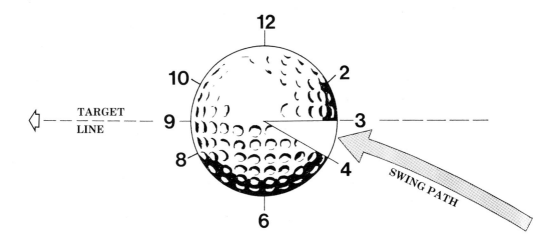

The Golf Swing

Stage 1

First let us look at what you should try to achieve. You should not worry too much about detail, but get an overall feel to the swing.

You want to swing the club in a large circle around yourself, keeping your eye on the ball and your head fairly steady. As you swing the club back allow your weight to go onto the right foot, but make this a smooth action or else you might swing back too far. Your body will turn as your arms swing, and the club should be swung so that it does not go too far past the horizontal over your shoulders.

Now swing your arms down, so that you swing through the ball allowing your weight to go onto your left foot. Your right heel must rise so that just your tip-toes are on the ground, and your body and head are facing the target. Do not keep your eyes fixed on where the ball was as this will stop you swinging through correctly.

It is good practice to start with just trying to brush the turf, then put a tee peg in the ground as your target. This will help you to think about swinging the club, and not just hitting the ball.

The correct grip and address position will take care of many of the technical aspects of the swing. To start with it is important to learn to make a balanced swing, always holding the finish for the count of three. As a young player you have great ability to mimic, so try to watch good players, then try to imitate what you have seen.

Stage 2

As you progress, you can become more specific about the swing. Certain movements may need correcting and should be practised in isolation, but then incorporated into the swing as a whole.

I have highlighted several very important check points at different stages of the swing, and you should take some time to work on them. Practise a good halfway back position until it becomes second nature. Check the top of your swing in a mirror, or on video, and also take note if you are balanced at the completion of your swing.

It is also important that you get a clear picture of what you are trying to achieve as you swing the club. Ideally the club will swing back and approach the ball from just inside the target line. To give you a better picture of this, imagine the ball has a clockface on it, you are trying to contact the ball in the 3-4 o'clock zone.

As you address the ball, remain relaxed and do not allow your hands, arms or shoulders to become tense. If a pre-shot waggle helps to keep you relaxed, then use that as part of your address drill.

The Golf Swing

The swing is a pivot, turning the shoulders round an imaginary pole down your back from your neck to a spot between your feet. In the picture on the left you turn right – not swaying but turning. Below the golfer pivots left to the correct finishing position. Try this exercise with a club behind your neck. It will teach you the correct positions.

The Golf Swing

The Backswing

To start the backswing, you should swing your arms and start to turn your shoulders as one movement, the hands at this point doing nothing more than holding the club. If this movement is made correctly, the club head will stay fairly close to the ground for the first foot or so of the backswing, and will start to swing on a gently curving path inside the target line.

As the swing progresses, stop the action when your hands have reached waist height, because here we can make some important checks.

The back of the left hand, and palm of the right should face forwards, i.e. parallel to the target line, the leading edge of the club (bottom groove) will also be parallel to the horizon and the toe of the club will be in the air.

Your shoulders will have continued to turn and their action will have encouraged the hips to have started to turn. The right knee flex must be as it was at address.

The left arm should still be fairly straight, but the right elbow must

The take away should be smooth, swinging the club on a gently curving path inside the target-line.

The Golf Swing

fold slightly to enable the hands and club face to be square at this point.

Your wrists will have started to cock upwards, and to check if you are in the correct position, turn your feet and body round to face the club, put the club head on the ground, and you should be in your address position.

Your wrists will have cocked correctly if the left thumb has flexed towards the inside of the left forearm, creating creases at the base of the left thumb, not at the back of the left wrist.

From that waist-high position, continue swinging the arms up as the body turns.

At the top of the backswing, the shoulders will have turned ninety degrees, and the hips about forty-five. The left arm should be slightly bowed, not absolutely straight and the right elbow should point towards the ground. The wrists will have continued to cock due to the swinging weight of the club head, but be sure that the last three fingers of the left hand are not allowed to loosen. They have to remain firmly on the grip, or else you will loose control.

Ideally the club shaft will be horizontal, the club head pointing at the target. The leading edge of the club should be parallel to the left forearm. This is a square position, and will help you to hit the ball consistently straight.

The right leg should still have its original flex although the knee may have moved slightly. About eighty per cent of your weight should be on this leg, with more towards the heel than the toe. Most youngsters are flexible, which means that the left heel should not rise too much if at all. If it does come up too much you will lose the coiling effect that is needed

A good position halfway back – the left arm is still fairly straight and the shoulders have turned. The left foot is still on the ground. Note the club face position.

The Golf Swing

for power.

One very good exercise for improving your turn, and to appreciate how your body should coil in the backswing, is to place a club behind your shoulders, angle forward from the hips, then put your feet apart. Now turn to the right, and you will naturally make the correct turn that we need in golf (see page 32).

Then turn to the left, letting the right heel come up completely. This simulates the correct through swing, providing that, once again, you keep the angle of your spine bent forward.

Because the shoulders must complete a 90° turn each way, you can see

why it is so important to have the chin up. If it was resting on the chest this turn would have been impossible.

Many juniors swing the club too far on the backswing, often because lack of strength prevents them controlling it properly. Also in an effort to hit the ball hard, the backswing becomes too fast for them to control the club, so guard against swinging too quickly. Do not swing it faster than you can control it.

Get somebody to check your position at the top of the backswing, or better still try to see your swing on video; seeing is believing, and will help you to quickly correct any errors.

Top of the backswing – the body has turned on its pivot, the head is steady and the back is facing the target.

The Downswing

From this powerful backswing position, the downswing begins. Slow motion video would tell us that as the arms and body are completing their backswing movement, the legs have already begun the downswing. Whilst in the professional and very strong golfer this is true, it is not necessarily what the beginner must think of.

So, what does start the downswing?

On the backswing your right side turned and your arms swung up-

This turning exercise will help you feel how a good turn should be made.

wards. Now reverse that procedure, so that your arms swing downwards and allow their action to bring your body square to the target line at impact. As the arms swing down, your weight must transfer smoothly onto the left leg. This action is very similar to the way you would skim a stone across water.

Many beginners tend to move the right shoulder out, i.e. towards the ball to start the downswing, because this is the part of them that they feel has most power.

Believe me, this is the wrong movement and will produce no power in the shot. Swing your arms, and let them control your body action.

If you concentrate on the arms swinging, it will help prevent you "casting", or throwing the club

Starting the downswing – the hips begin to turn as the left arm pulls down.

The Golf Swing

head with your hands. This is a common mistake, but again will waste power and cause very inaccurate shots.

In an effort to mimic the impact position of the golfing stars, many juniors use far too much leg action at the start of the downswing, which prevents them using their arms and hands powerfully enough in the swing. Instead they create a weak swing with an open club face which makes the ball slice to the right.

Match the speed of your arm swing with the smooth transfer of weight onto your left side and this will create a chain reaction of good movements in your swing.

As the hands approach the impact area they will add some power to the swing. The wrist cock you created on the backswing is now going to unwind and, providing you are not gripping too tightly, you will then get maximum club head speed at impact. Have the feeling that you are hitting the ball with the right hand, allowing the right hand and forearm to start to turn over the left through impact. Feel that you are directing the club head down the target line. At this point in the swing your shoulders will

The downswing – note how the arms swing down as the weight transfers to the left foot.

be virtually parallel to the target line, while your hips will be starting to face the target, allowing your arms to swing through unimpeded. Imagine that as the right hand hits the ball, the right knee moves towards the left.

This action will make you hit through the ball, not at it. Keep your head steady at this point, try to see the club hit the ball. By the time the hands are through to waist height, the right arm will straighten, while the left is folding. This really is a mirror image of the same position in the backswing.

As the swing continues your body is pulled round towards the target by your arms, and the head should rotate, so that at the finish you face the target. Your weight should be mainly on the left foot, with the right heel off the ground, the foot balanced on the toes.

The momentum of the swing means that the club will finish over your left shoulder. Try to imagine that your hands finish at the same height as they were at the top of the backswing.

When viewed face on your spine should be straight, with your head above the left foot. Too many youngsters get into what is called the reverse "C" position, where the spine is arched back – this is not only inju-

Impact – the hands are slightly ahead of the ball, the weight is on the left side and the head is over the ball – still in position.

rious to the spine, but useless in the swing. As you swing through allow your head to feel as though it moves **towards** the target after impact, not backwards.

If you face the target and look at the swing of a good player, most of the spinal angle set at address should still be evident at the completion of the swing, so that the player's right shoulder is lower than the left.

Good balance is so important, and the photograph on page 28 shows the finish position of Frank Nobilo, the popular New Zealander, hitting a 5-iron.

Note how he has his body turned to finish facing the target.

He has very good technique and swing within his particular ability, probably at eighty to ninety percent of their power. Use him as your guide and try to mimic him. Don't try to swing with 100% of your power – you will only lose balance and thus accuracy and distance.

For many young players, if the address position is good, the backswing will be good; if from that position, they think of swinging through to a balanced finish, then many of the movements I have described will happen naturally. It is only if you are not playing well that you may need to

Note how the hands have 'released' – the right hand rolling over the left to square the club-face and add power. The right knee has kicked in towards the left but the eyes are still focussed on where the ball was.

check your swing to find out just where the fault is occurring.

The art of hitting the ball well is to time the leg, arm, hands and body action to produce a square club face at impact. If you consistently slice the ball, i.e. it curves to the right, the club face is open at impact. If your grip is correct, then your leg action is too strong for your arm and hand action. Hit some shots with your feet together, and this will help you focus on your hand action.

If you consistently hook the ball, i.e. it curves to the left, then the club face is closed at impact. If your grip is not too strong, then you need to speed up your leg action. Try to make a slightly stronger move with the right knee through impact, which will clear your left side, preventing you from closing the club face so quickly.

As you develop more strength the timing in your swing must change accordingly. Your hands and arms will gradually start to create more speed, and your leg action must alter to accommodate this.

Remember, to hit the ball further, you must hit it better, not just faster.

A perfect finish – facing the target, balanced, with the right foot on tip-toe. The spine is still at the same angle as at address.

The Golf Swing

The Plane

The club head is swung in a circle which, in golfing terms, is called the arc. The angle on which the arc is inclined is called the plane, and is best viewed when looking at the golfer towards the target.

The plane is governed by the length of the club, which determines how far away from the ball you stand, and how far forward the spine is tilted (called the posture.) Providing you adopt the method already described, angling forward from the hips, you will encourage the correct plane.

Because the shorter clubs make you bend forward more, you stand closer to the ball with the hands quite near to the thighs. This makes the plane upright.

Because the woods have longer shafts you do not bend forward so much and stand further away from the ball, with the hands further from the thigh. This makes the plane flatter.

You do not need to think about altering the plane as this is done by the change in address.

Now we shall go through the various stages of the swing again, though do always remember that it is just one movement.

Because of the length of shaft and the address position adopted, the driver will be swung on a flatter plane than the wedge.

The Golf Swing

Set-up   Take-away   Halfway Back   Top of the backswing

The Golf Swing

Into the downswing   *Impact*   *Release*   *Finish*

Don't sway on the backswing.

The club face has been swung too flat and the club is open.

Swing the club back – don't pick it up.

Keep a firm grip on the backswing – don't let your little finger "play the flute".

Fault Finder

The right leg should not be this straight at the top of the backswing.

"Casting" – throwing the right shoulder out makes you hit out-to-in.

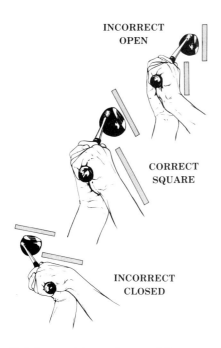

INCORRECT
OPEN

CORRECT
SQUARE

INCORRECT
CLOSED

Club face position at the top of the backswing – the correct one is in the centre.

Too much leg action causes the club face to be open – a slice often results.

Power v Accuracy

Colin Montgomerie demonstrates power.

Power v Accuracy

Problems in rough.

Every golfer dreams of the day when he or she can stand on the first tee and drive the ball 280 yards straight down the middle. Most professionals would like to be able to do the same thing every time too.

Reality is, as so often, quite different. Very few golfers, even top professionals, will achieve that distance and accuracy off the first tee, though no doubt they will work up to it as they go through their round.

Although the top players regularly drive well over 250 yards (with a good bounce and forward roll of the ball) a day at any golf tournament will clearly show that they are not all as accurate as they would like to be.

The average golfer will obviously hit less distance than this – younger golfers just do not have the physical strength to hit the ball a long way until they are in their mid-teens when the body's muscles begin to generate the sort of power required.

Of course it is great fun and very exhilerating to out-hit your friends but, so often, in a search for power, the previously evident good movements in the swing can be lost. Do not fall into the trap of gaining inaccurate power, because the name of this game is how many, not how far.

At an early age and for those just beginning golf, accuracy is, however, possible by swinging the club correctly.

The question often asked then is: which is best – power or accuracy?

For any golfer beginning the game, accuracy is, without doubt, the thing

Problems in trees.

Power v Accuracy

to aim for.

It's interesting to watch senior golfers and ladies play, for although many of them lack the physical strength to be able to blast the ball down the fairway any great distance, they almost always knock it straight down the middle. Anyone playing straight stands a much better chance of beating the long-hitting but wayward golfer.

Not only does the straight hitter keep the ball in play all the time, rather than being in the trees, the rough, or even out-of-bounds, but he or she will feel better for doing so.

The great Harry Vardon, six times winner of the Open championship, learnt to play his golf on a course which had narrow fairways. He had to be accurate even though he was not the longest hitter of his time. Despite being regularly out-driven, he was rarely beaten.

Also, if you look logically at a long hole like a 480 yard par-5, you have three shots to reach the green. The average man would stand on the tee and try to hit a big tee-shot. Watch at any golf club and you will see a fair number of men failing to reach the green in three.

Yet a par-5 does not need a huge tee shot. A 480-yarder needs three easy shots of 160 yards each, within the capabilities of all but the youngest golfers.

So, back to the question – distance or accuracy?

The answer must be accuracy. Distance will be built up over time, but learn to keep the ball straight and you won't go far wrong in golf.

Straight down the middle.

Pro Quote

Ronan Rafferty

Born in Northern Ireland in 1964 Ronan Rafferty spent much of his boyhood practising at the Warrenpoint Golf Club. In 1979 he won the British Boys' Championship and the Irish Youths' Championship, also playing for his country in other events, including the Eisenhower Trophy in 1980. The same year he won the Irish Amateur Championship and tied for the English Open Strokeplay Championship. He was also the youngest player ever to play in the Walker Cup, in 1981, aged 17.

Turning professional shortly after that he played for his country in the World Cup and Dunhill Cup. 1989 saw him win the European Tour Order of Merit with three titles and a handful of top-ten finishes. In the 1989 Ryder Cup he defeated Mark Calcavecchia, then Open Champion, in the singles.

"I think it is important to have the right equipment, from the very beginning. I see too many players, of all ages, playing with golf clubs that are just not suitable for them – either the shafts are too stiff, the grips are the wrong size or the club just does not suit them.

"Also, don't try to use a driver when you can hit the ball better with a 3-wood or, when young, a 5-wood. Get good with the easier clubs first, then move onto the others. Make it easy.

"Make sure you talk to your club professional and get him to match the golf equipment to you – not the other way round. Without the correct clubs you won't play good golf."

Ronan Rafferty on the tee.

On The Tee

Each hole starts with a tee shot played from within the markers, and up to two club lengths back of them. Always choose a smooth area both to stand on and to swing in.

It is entirely wrong to think that you must use a driver; in fact most golfers young and old would score far better without one. The driver has the least loft of all clubs, and therefore puts more sidespin on the ball. This is the spin that causes the ball to curve to the right or left. Because a 3-wood or a 5-wood has more loft, it will put more backspin and less sidespin on the ball than the driver.

As you become more proficient you can start to use the driver, but beginners should tee off with a 5- or 3-wood and concentrate on hitting the ball accurately into the fairway.

As already mentioned, find a smooth and even part of the tee, and tee the ball up so that the top half of the ball is above the top of the club face.

If there is an area of trouble on one side of the fairway, such as a lake or trees, or perhaps out of bounds, tee up on the *same side* as the trouble. For example, if there is out of bounds on the left side of the fairway, tee up on the left, as this will encourage you to hit away from the trouble.

The ball is positioned forward of centre in your stance, so that it is inside your left heel. Put a little more weight on your right foot, and keep your head behind the ball. This will give you the feeling of looking at the back of the ball.

You need your widest stance when hitting from the tee, but guard against too wide a stance in an effort

Teeing area – you can move back but not forward of the markers.

to get power. This will just restrict your leg action and turn. A good guide is to stand the width of your walking pace.

From this address position you will be able to hit the ball when the club head is just starting its upward swing. Do not try to hit the ball any harder than you would for a 7-iron. Don't swing fast in an effort to gain distance.

On the backswing try to keep the club head low until it passes your right foot, then you will create a good shoulder turn. Swing through the ball so that you finish balanced on your left side. Always hold that position for the count of three.

You must trust the golf club to create the extra length in the shot, and do not fall into the trap of trying to hit the ball flat out. Of course you must accelerate through the ball, but maintain your balance, and do not make the mistake of many golfers who, in an effort to put too much power into the shot, almost fall over. To help with the rhythm, say to yourself very slowly, "Swing the club", the word "club" coinciding with the strike.

Have a mental picture of one of the world's best golfers, perhaps Nick Faldo, or Ballesteros, because they have such good balance.

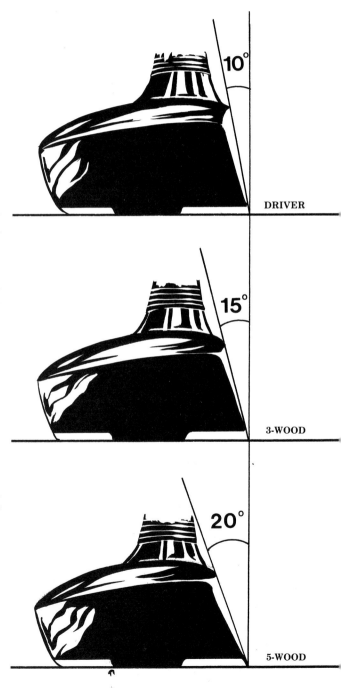

The different lofts of a Driver (top), 3-wood (centre) and 5-wood (bottom). Because of the lack of loft, most golfers find the Driver difficult. Hitting a 3 or 5-wood off the tee increases confidence as the ball flies higher.

On The Tee

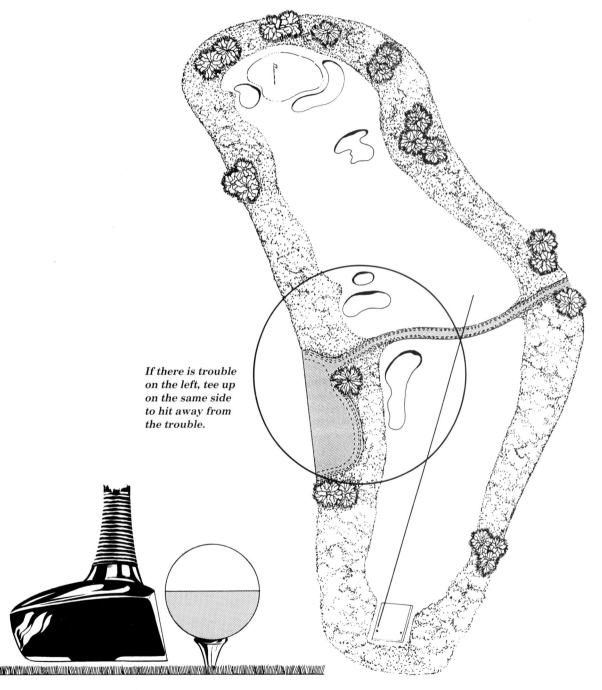

If there is trouble
on the left, tee up
on the same side
to hit away from
the trouble.

*Ball height on the tee – the 'equator' of the
ball is level with the top of the club-head.*

Hitting away from trouble.

Major Faults

To hit the drive your maximum distance, the club head must approach from inside the target line, so it contacts the ball in the 3 to 4 o'clock zone. This will ensure that the club head approaches the ball from what is called a shallow angle of attack. That is to say it will hit the ball when the club head is swinging along parallel to the ground.

Many golfers are unable to hit the ball like this because of a set-up fault. As the ball is played nearer to the left foot than for irons, it is very easy for the shoulders to start to aim to the left.

This will cause you to make a backswing where the club does not swing inside the target line but outside. When the club approaches the ball it will be on the outside in the 2 to 3 o'clock zone and from a steep angle of attack. That means you will chop down on the ball rather than sweeping it away. Very often you will sky the shot, and will have telltale marks on the top edge of the club. You will also hit shots that go to the left then curve to the right – a slice. This is not a powerful shot and will lose you valuable yards.

When set-up correctly, your right shoulder will be lower than your left. Have a friend place a club across your shoulders to check that they are square, or even a little closed. Imagine that your club head is like an aeroplane taking off and landing. It will travel along the runway parallel to the ground before take off and landing. It does not shoot straight up in the air, or approach the runway steeply, when coming down.

Even from a good set-up you might make a powerless swing by simply just swinging your arms. You must have a good body turn, and the club across the shoulders drill detailed earlier will help you to develop this. In the back swing, be sure to keep the club head low until it has passed your right foot; this will help you to turn.

The other major fault occurs because the player uses the body too much rather than the arms. In an effort to create power from the top of the backswing they move their head towards the target. This prevents the release of the golf club through impact, pushing weakly at the ball, often slicing it right and short.

From the top of the backswing, keep your head behind the ball until your arms swing through and pull your body and head round to face the target.

The key to good driving is the correct set-up, followed by a good turn where the weight transfers onto the right side, in the backswing. Keep the head behind the ball and swing through smoothly to a balanced finish. Let the ball get in the way of the good swing – do not hit at it.

Fault Finder

Right: Fault – shoulders open. The club swing-path will follow the line of the shoulders, bringing the club head out-to-in across the ball; this normally causes a slice, or a pull.

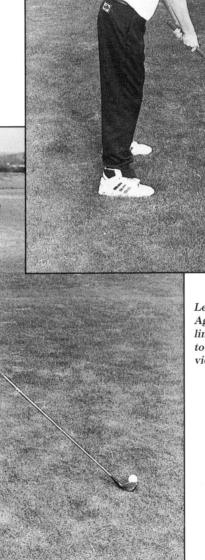

Left: Fault – shoulders closed. Again the club will follow the line of the shoulders, moving in-to-out, which normally causes a violent hook left, or push right.

Right: Fault – reverse 'C' – the spine is too arched.

Above: Fault – moving laterally towards target.

Right: Fault – trying to hit ball up.

Pro Quote

Seve Ballesteros

Seve Ballesteros began playing golf at a very early age, caddying at a local course in northern Spain when he was about six. His three elder brothers also caddied and, just before dark, they would sneak onto the deserted course well out of sight of the club-house and play a few holes, Seve using just one club – an old 3-iron.

His interest in golf grew and he spent hours just hitting a ball with that one old club, building up his golfing muscles and learning to shape shots with just the single club, closing it for long shots and opening the face to get height on the ball. Those years spent with that one club helped him to become one of the world's best players at conjuring up shots that no other player would attempt.

He arrived on the European Tour in 1973. In 1976 he began the British Open with rounds of 69, 69, before tieing joint 2nd with Jack Nicklaus. He won the Open in 1979, 1984 and 1988, adding the US Masters in 1980 and 1983.

"Well, I would say that it is vital to practise everything, non-stop. Some people think you should practise just one part of the game, like the short game, but I insist that you must practise all parts of the game, including putting, to become a good player. No part of your game should be better than any other."

Bernhard Langer hits a shot from the fairway.

On The Fairway

Let us imagine that you have hit your drive nicely down the fairway and the ball is sitting up on a cushion of grass.

If you still have a long way to the green, you can hit the 5-wood. If you find the length of this club rather daunting it is quite acceptable to grip down the shaft so that an inch or so protrudes from your left hand. This will give you more control and is worth sacrificing a little length.

Set-up with the ball just forward of centre so that you can sweep the ball off the turf. The weight is even on each foot, and you should try to keep the club head low to the ground as you start the backswing. Do not let the distance you still have to hit the ball to the green cause you to make an over aggressive swing. As a beginner you are just trying to keep the ball in play, and to progress steadily. Remember what we said earlier about accuracy being more important than distance.

If the lie is very good, the more experienced golfer could use the 3-wood, providing that a mis-hit will not result in disaster.

Everyone will hit the clubs different distances, depending on your age and strength, and until such time as you perfect the strike, which comes with practice, the distance with the same club will vary from shot to shot, based on how well you hit it.

Apart from the driver, which is very difficult to use off the fairway, the 3-wood goes furthest, followed by the 5-wood, then the irons, the lowest numbers going furthest.

So after two shots, let us imagine that we are 120 yards from the flag. You may need to hit your 5-iron. Play the ball fairly centrally in your stance, so that you can hit it whilst the club head is still travelling downwards.

It is most important that you understand that with an iron shot the ball will go in the air providing that it is hit a descending blow. Many youngsters try to hit the ball UP into the air, falling back onto their right foot, only to see the ball roll along the ground. From this result, they believe

Golf is a game of opposites. If you hit down, the club puts backspin on the ball and it goes up.

they did not hit it upwards enough, and the next shot is topped along the ground even more.

As the club descends into the ball, it is the loft on the club that puts backspin on the ball, and this gets it airborne. To hit the ball up, you must hit down.

If the ball is struck correctly with your irons, you will take a divot, or remove the top layer of grass after hitting the ball. This is the result of the downward strike, and helps to prove good contact was made. If you fail to take even a small divot or some grass, particularly with your short irons, this will indicate a fault. Although you should always carefully replace divots

Set-up for iron – note that the spine is straight but angled forward.

(except on the tee) never be afraid of taking one.

So with a narrower stance than for your tee-shot, set-up square to your target, ball central and weight even. Have a picture in your mind of the club head descending onto the ball as you swing through. If you simply just hit down on the ball, without swinging through, you will probably hit it fat, i.e. hit the ground before the ball. So imagine that your arms and hands swing the club head down into the back of the ball as you swing onto the left side. The finish again is so important, balanced mainly on the left side, right heel up, body and head facing the target.

Iron shots are hit while the club head is still descending. For fairway wood shots, play the ball about 1 inch further forward in your stance, and sweep the ball from the turf.

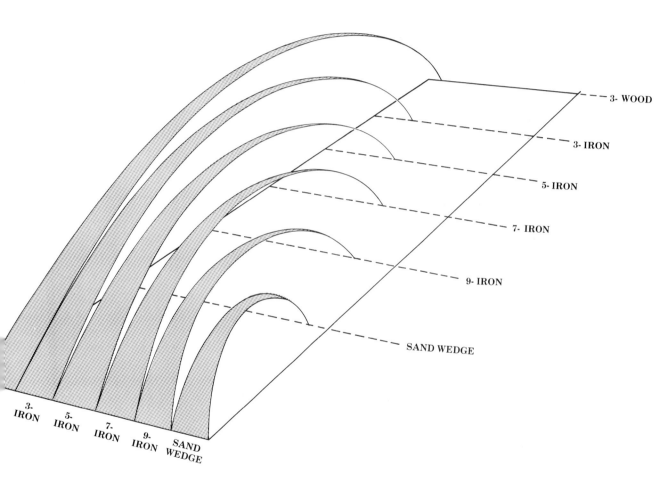

3- WOOD

3- IRON

5- IRON

7- IRON

9- IRON

SAND WEDGE

3-IRON 5-IRON 7-IRON 9-IRON SAND WEDGE

The woods and longer irons hit the ball further. The sand wedge is the shortest club in the bag, in its actual length as well as the distance it hits the ball.

Approaching perfection

Perfect approach shots keep your scores down.

Approaching perfection

Whilst all parts of golf from the drive to the putt are important, perhaps the most satisfying aspect of the game is to be a good approach player with the ability to hit shots from 100 yards out or so to a position very close to the pin.

It is on these approach shots that birdies (or net birdies if the stroke index gives you a shot) are made; professionals would be looking to get these "stone dead" – that is so close to the hole as to make the putt virtually a formality.

Seeing a shot from 100 yards or so out fly high over bunkers and land securely on the green within single putting distance of the hole is wonderfully satisfying – and demoralising for any opponent who still has to play a difficult shot!

The main point about these shots is that they don't need power, just pinpoint accuracy, so younger golfers and those who do not hit so far should be able to reach a high standard in this department of the game.

We shall be dealing with playing from bunkers and rough later on in this book (pages 68 to 81) so for the moment we shall assume that all our shots are from the fairway – hope-

Set-up for a pitch over bunker – weight is on the left side (left) and the takeaway is much steeper (right) than for a normal shot. This helps you to hit down more on the ball, getting it up faster.

fully, having learnt from the earlier parts of this book that is the ONLY place you will hit your shots anyway!

There is not just one way to play approach shots. It depends very much on several factors: are there bunkers in the way, or perhaps a lake or stream in front of the green?; is the green on a plateau or in a dip?; is it windy or wet?; is the approach flat so that we could just run the ball along the ground like a very long putt?

Because an approach shot is not so long it does not mean that you shouldn't hit it hard. Too many higher-handicap players leave their approach shots well short of the pin – quite often short of the green itself. The primary reason for this is not that they have chosen the wrong club (though that can be a factor) but that they have not hit it fully. On approach shots, don't under-hit the ball. There is nothing wrong with going past the flag.

Also, try to think about where you would most like to putt from. If the green slopes it is normally easier putting up-hill than down. But, if that

means going over a bunker, or perilously close to a water hazard near the green, play safe – go for the fat part of the green rather than firing the shot directly at the pin.

The Short Irons

If you finish short of the green, say 60 yards, then use a more lofted club, perhaps a 9-iron or pitching wedge. With these clubs, take a narrower stance, with your feet and hips just a little open, but shoulders square to the target line. Put slightly more weight on the left side, and keep the ball central in the stance.

This set-up will help you to swing your arms up in the backswing so that the strike is slightly more descending than with the medium irons. There is not too much emphasis on body action, or weight transference, although some does occur. The ball will easily rise up into the air, and it will not roll very much when it lands.

This shot becomes more difficult when you are so close to the green

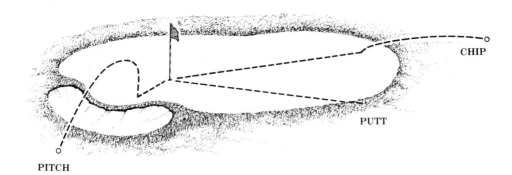

Pitch when you have to get the ball over a hazard. Chip when you want to get the ball on the green and rolling. Putt whenever you can.

that less than a full swing is needed. To help lessen the power, grip down the shaft, and make your backswing just three-quarters of its normal length.

Only by practice will you be able to judge just how hard to hit these shots, so initially concentrate on hitting the ball correctly.

Chipping

Once you are within a few yards of the green, with no bunker to go over, you can play a chip shot, which lofts the ball over the small amount of fringe grass onto the green, then lets it run up to the hole. This shot can be played with almost any iron in the bag, depending on the situation, but to begin with you can use the 7 or 8.

2. ...on the backswing the 'Y' of the arms and club stays in place...

1. When you are going to chip the ball the hands should be ahead of the ball...

3. ...as it does on the short follow-through. Keep the wrists firm throughout the stroke.

Approaching perfection

The idea is that the ball lands on the green because you can be more sure of an even bounce.

Set-up with a narrow stance, feet and hips open, shoulders square. The ball is played centrally in the stance, or even just back of centre, with more weight on the left foot than the right, and hands forward. Grip down the club, then make a swing where the wrists remain firm. Just try to swing the forearms back and through and the loft on the club will just pop the ball over the fringe onto the green. The best way to think about this shot is that it is like putting with a lofted club. Just swing the V formed by the forearms, and the shot is simple.

With experience you can vary the choice of club; a 5 or 6-iron will only slightly loft the ball into the air, and it will run quite a distance. This is ideal if you are just off the fringe and the pin is at the back of the green. If you are further off the green with the hole cut quite near, then a 9-iron or even the wedge may be more suitable, as the ball spends more time in the air and does not run much.

Pitching

If you have to loft the ball over a bunker or a rough area of grass, this is called pitching. You can use the wedge or sand wedge, depending on the lie and your ability.

The beginner should not use the sand iron, as this may be too heavy to control and because of its design it might literally bounce off the grass and cause you to top the ball.

The shot can be played quite adequately with the pitching wedge or even a 9-iron if that is your most lofted club. The set up is just the same as for shots from the fairway with the short irons, but it is the fact that it is a very short shot that makes it difficult to judge, because you only need a part swing. Whilst the chip is played with firm wrists, in pitching a little wrist action is developed helping to create backspin and height on the shot.

With the weight on your left side, grip down the club, have the ball central in a narrow open stance, but shoulders square. Swing your arms up and down picturing the club descending onto the ball.

Most bad pitches are hit because the player tries to hit the ball UP into the air. Rely on the club's loft; as you swing through just let your knees move a little towards the target. Do not look up too soon but keep looking at the spot where the ball was for as long as you dare.

Round The Green Strategy

When you are just off the green, always take the easiest option.

It is easier to putt than chip, and it is easier to chip than pitch.

Providing the ground is not too rough or the grass long and wet, by all means use the putter; the shot is easier to judge; and a bad putt will be better than a bad chip. If the ground will not allow you to putt, then chip, keeping the wrists firm, and only as a last resort attempt the more difficult pitching action.

Pro Quote

Brett Ogle

Brett Ogle was a relative late-comer to golf, not learning to play until he was about 15. Before that he was very keen on other sports, including athletics, swimming and rugby. Turning professional he played the Australian and Asian Tours before coming to Europe to expand his experience. In his third year in Europe he shot a 61 at the Madrid Open, setting a course record, but only gaining him third place. Two weeks later, at another tournament he lost four balls on the front nine of the Benson & Hedges.

He is, though, becoming ever more consistent and in 1991 was the fifth longest hitter on Tour overall, and in the top 20 for greens hit in regulation, proof of his prowess in accuracy and distance.

"I think I took up golf a little too late, really," he says. "Eight or nine years old is the ideal time.

"Golf helps you mature much faster than other sports – it's so much a game played in the mind – it really helps you grow up and find yourself. Yet at the same time, unlike tennis, for example, you won't get that early burn out, because there is not so much stress and strain on your heart as in more physically demanding sports.

"I think it's vital that you should enjoy golf – play a lot on the course to get to know the situations you will meet, but you do also need to practise a lot, making it as much fun as you can.

"Throw a lot of golf balls around in an area, into the rough, in bunkers, on slopes, into divots – then hit each one of them, learning to play from difficult lies rather than having every ball sitting up perfectly.

"That way, you'll have more fun and won't get bored. Good luck to you all."

Hazards

Professionals show just how easy it is to get out of bunkers.

Hazards

Every golfer, at any age, hates hitting the ball into the rough, the trees, or a bunker. The chances of doing so are, however, pretty high so it is vital to learn how to get out of trouble if you are to save shots on the golf course.

Bunkers:

Most amateur golfers have a terrible fear of bunkers, yet most professionals would rather be in a bunker than in the surrounding areas, proof if it were needed that, once mastered, the bunker shot is one of the easiest in golf.

Watch any tournament on television and you will see the top players splashing the ball out of the sand to positions often just a few inches from the hole, to rapturous applause from an admiring crowd.

There are, basically, three types of bunker shot, the splash shot, the buried or "plugged" lie, and the long bunker shot.

The Splash Shot

This is the shot played from greenside bunkers, where the ball sits up on a cushion of sand.

First of all, you should use your sand iron, since it was designed many years ago – by the American golfer Gene Sarazen – to make bunker shots easy! It has a metal flange or bounce on the sole, which prevents the club digging too deeply into the sand. Instead it encourages the club to take

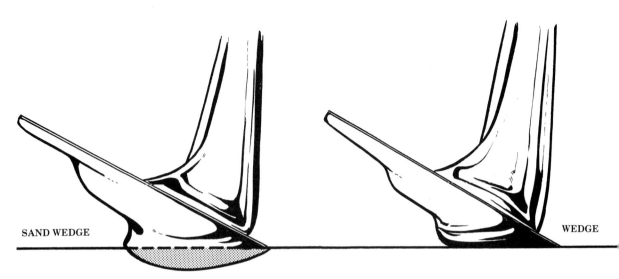

SAND WEDGE

WEDGE

A sand iron has a 'flange' which helps it bounce off sand rather than digging in. An ordinary pitching wedge (right) has a flatter sole.

a shallow divot of sand from beneath the ball, that sand being tossed out of the bunker, the ball with it. If you do not have a sand wedge, use the pitching wedge, the next most-lofted club in the bag.

To bring the flange into full operation, you must hold the club face open, the club face itself almost pointing skywards. This puts more loft on the club and thus gets the ball up faster. First, turn the club a little to the right, then take your grip. For more control grip down the club a little, which will also make the club feel lighter. In a bunker it is a penalty if you touch the sand with your club prior to the shot, so you may feel safer taking your grip outside the bunker.

When you set up, instead of having your body parallel to the target line, you should stand with your shoulders, hip, knees and feet open, i.e. aimed to the left. The club face should aim at

The bunker splash-shot. Stand open to the target and swing the club on the body-line, not the ball to target line. This will cut across the ball, splashing it out of the sand.

Hazards

the target, or even a little to the right of it.

The ball is positioned opposite the left instep, with about 60-70 per cent of the weight on the left side. The inside of the heels are about twelve inches apart. Wriggle your feet into the sand for a firm footing, which will also help you assess the texture and quantity of the sand in the bunker (it often being necessary to hit harder when the sand is hard or wet, less so when it is dry and powdery). The hands are just ahead of the club face, and the club is held about one or two inches above the sand.

Many players make the mistake of holding the club too near the ball. Your object for this shot is not to hit the ball, but a point about two inches behind it, so let the club hover above this point and focus on that and not the ball.

From this set-up, you will swing

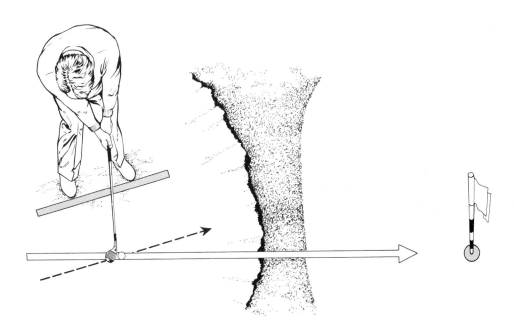

Bunker Splash-shot.
Note how the feet (and thus the body) are aligned left of the target. The club, swung along the same line, cuts under the ball and lands it softly on the green.

Hazards

along your shoulder line, which in effect makes you cut fairly steeply across the target line from out to in.

You should feel that you make the swing mainly by swinging your arms up in the backswing, with little thought about turning your body. Be sure to swing back until your hands are at least shoulder height, or you will probably not generate enough club head speed to get through the sand.

There is very little weight transference in the backswing.

As you swing the club down into the sand, feel your weight swinging onto your left side, but do not let your right hand roll over the left. Have the image of keeping the back of the left hand facing the sky as you swing through to a full finish, body facing the target.

Most bad shots are hit because the player slows down into the shot, or falls back onto the right foot in an effort to hit the ball UP into the air. Imagine the ball has legs, and you must swing down under the ball to chop the legs off; cruel to golf balls but good for the score!

Make sure you don't fall into either of these bad habits. Take a long enough backswing and hit through. At first you may hit some bad shots because you hit the ball before the sand, but practice will make you more proficient at hitting the sand first.

You will find it helpful to practise without a ball, concentrating solely on striking the sand accurately. Draw two lines in the sand about 6 inches apart, and with the right hand line inside the left heel, practise removing the sand between the two lines. This will clearly show you how accurate you are.

Once you are confident of getting the ball out, then you can refine the length of the shot by varying the power, but learn one shot to start with, and gain confidence.

Long Bunker Shots

If you hit the ball into a fairway bunker, providing it is sitting up quite well, you can still play a long shot.

First you must decide which club to use, based on how high a lip the ball has to clear. The worst shot to hit is one where the ball hits the bunker-face and drops back in the bunker, so be very careful with your choice of club. If you think you can play a 6-iron to carry the correct distance, hit a 7-iron instead just to be safe.

It is essential that you hit the ball first and not one single grain of sand, so position the ball back in your stance just behind where you would normally play an iron shot. Wriggle your feet slightly into the sand, but not too much, and grip down the club about one inch.

Balance and keeping a firm footing are now all you need think about, so swing very smoothly, focusing on the back of the ball, and make your normal swing. Full power is not advised, since you may slip, so take it easy.

If you are not successful at this shot, it is advisable to use the sand-iron and play a normal splash shot. Getting out at the first attempt must be the aim.

Plugged Lie

When the ball sits well down in the sand, usually in its own pitch mark, it is called a plugged lie.

Since the ball is lower in the sand, you must get the club head deeper into the sand in order to get the ball out. To help this happen play the shot with the club face square, not open, so take your normal grip, with the leading edge square to the target.

Since the blade is square, you must set your body square, not open, so that a club across your shoulders would point to the target as out on the fairway.

With your weight on your left side, position the ball back of centre in your stance, which should be slightly wider than for the splash shot. This set-up will help you to get a really steep attack on the ball.

Cock your wrists early in the backswing, as you swing your arms up steeply. Focus on a point about one inch behind the ball, and think of hitting down into the sand. You will not be able to follow through very far, but the ball will come out quite readily.

Because the club face is square, and the ball back in your stance, there is not much loft on the club, so the ball tends to come out low, and runs on landing. So be careful where you aim this shot. If there is a high bunker face in front of you, or another bunker or a water hazard on the other side of the green, it may be better to aim away from the pin.

With all bunker shots the first target is to get out in one shot, so do not think it is defeatist either to aim sideways or even backwards – it isn't.

Bunker Practice

Although professionals make bunker shots look easy, they have practised many hours in order to reach

With the ball plugged in the sand, have the body and feet square to the target, just as you would for a normal fairway shot.

this standard.

Getting out of a bunker is easy, getting the ball close is much more difficult. Professionals will instinctively vary the amount they open the club face, their stance and the power of the swing, according to the lie of the ball, the sand texture and the distance required. However, once you are confident enough that you can get the ball out first time, every time, then you will be able to refine that action.

When bunker shots from good lies prove no problem, throw some balls into the bunker and play them as they lie. This will give you valuable experience so, when faced with that lie on the course, you will be better able to cope with it.

Bunker Etiquette

It is most essential that when you have played your ball out of the bunker you rake your footprints and the area you have played from. If there is no rake, then use your feet and the club to lightly smooth out the top of the sand. It will not take more than a few seconds, so think of others, (even if they have not raked the bunker) leaving it as you would wish to find it. The same goes for a practice bunker – leave it as you would hope to find it!

Please rake the bunker – every time! Thank you.

Bunkers

Try this practice routine to perfect your bunker play. Draw two lines in the sand (in a practice bunker) about four inches apart – don't worry about using a ball...

...then hit down through the two lines, trying not to hit the sand outside the lines. This will get you into the habit of hitting the sand behind the ball, which is essential if you are to splash it out on a cushion of sand.

Having a Rough Time

Getting out of the rough is your first priority.

Having a Rough Time

Apart from bunkers, most players, professional and amateur, hate playing out of the rough. Firstly, of course, it is because the previous shot has been a little wayward and, secondly, it is more difficult to hit a good shot from the rough – particularly the deep rough – than it is from a well manicured fairway.

The secret, as with bunker play, is to get out first time, every time. Golf is about the number of shots you take.

You can't SAVE shots – you can only stop WASTING them!

There are probably three types of situation you might find yourself in:-
1. light rough off the fairway;
2. deep rough;
3. light rough round a green.

For light rough you have an excellent chance of still making a good shot. For the second you really only have one sensible option – to get back out onto the fairway. The third is far

Good Lie (semi-rough) set-up – weight left, ball back in stance, hands well ahead of the ball.

more difficult, for you have to hit the ball hard enough to get out, but delicately enough to keep it on the green.

The first – light rough – is the easiest. Providing the ball is not down in a divot or other little dip in the ground you will probably be able to get a club at it fairly easily.

In light rough, with some distance to go to your target, a 5-wood or 7-wood could be the answer. Woods have a wide sole-plate, (unlike an iron) and will swish through the grass, parting it more easily than an iron.

In light rough you may be lucky enough to find the ball sitting up on a fluffy piece of grass. In this case, position the ball the same as for a wood shot from the fairway, (just about an inch further forward than for an iron shot). This will help you to hit the ball with a shallow attack, i.e. when the club is travelling horizontally rather than downwards. Make a smooth swing, sweeping the ball from the top of the grass, and you should hit a good shot.

If the ball is sitting down in the rough, play the ball more centrally, perhaps just back from a normal iron shot position, and put a little more weight on the left foot. This set-up will help you get a slightly steeper attack on the ball so that the club does not tangle with the grass too

much prior to hitting the ball. From this sort of lie, you must not be too greedy, so using a short iron could be the safest option to ensure you get out onto the fairway first time.

With all lies in the rough, have a couple of practice swings first – well away from the ball! This will prepare you for the effect the grass will have on the club head as you swing through.

In light rough, some way from the green, a 5-wood could be your best choice.

Having a Rough Time

In Deep

Now for the nasty stuff! When you are in deep rough you should have only one thought in mind – get back on the fairway immediately. Forget Seve and his amazing 200-yarders out of five-feet high jungle to an inch from the pin – you and I can't do it!

Your best friend in deep rough is your sand wedge, but even before you think about hitting the ball you should be out in the middle of the fairway looking for an ideal spot to land the ball so as to be in position from which to hit your next shot.

Then back to the ball. Take a slightly open stance, the club face pointing at your target – that is the

Take the club away steeply, the wrists cocked early. Then hit down hard, as you would in a bunker shot.

spot you have chosen to land the ball; have your weight about 60 – 70 per cent on your left foot so you are leaning slightly forwards, towards the target, with the ball back in your stance, as shown in the illustration. With your hands forward of the ball, swing your arms up steeply, cocking your wrists early in the backswing, then hit down sharply into the back of the ball or just behind it, exactly as you would in a bunker. Try to swing through, although in severe situations, the deep grass may prevent this. The ball should come out quite high, but will not travel very far. At least you are back in play, and with a little practice the shot is really quite simple.

In heavy rough set up with an open stance.

Having a Rough Time

As in a bunker, though, make sure you hit the ball hard enough – don't "quit" on the shot – that will only leave you still in the rough, with another shot gone.

Now for the tricky bit

On to those areas of rough, some light and some not so light, which surround most greens. The main problem here is that although you have to get the ball out of the rough, you also have to stop it fairly quickly, on the green.

These are very delicate shots and the dividing line between success and failure is very fine. It is always difficult to get any backspin to control the ball; sometimes the grass tends to make the shot fly, whilst at other times it dampens the force of the swing, and the ball barely trickles out.

Usually the best clubs to use are the sand iron or wedge, depending on the lie and the shot required. Try to imagine how the ball will fly and where it needs to land in order to finish near (or even in) the hole.

The lie of the ball will determine your choice of shot; if it is good you can play a high soft floater, but from a poor lie the ball will come out lower and run more on landing.

For the first shot – which will land "softly" and stop fairly quickly – line up open to the target with the club face pointing at the target, your weight more on the left foot, and the ball fairly forward in your stance. The cushion of grass beneath the ball will enable you to slide the club – a sand iron for maximum height – under the ball without much trouble.

You do not need to swing the club too steeply in the backswing, instead think of swinging smoothly back and through the same amount. As you finish, try to keep the back of the left hand facing the sky, which will hold the club face square through the shot, as recommended for bunkers. Always resist the temptation to look up too soon, instead keep your eyes firmly fixed on the ground for an extra second or two.

The secret is to have a slow, smooth swing. It is primarily the length of the swing which dictates the distance the ball travels, not how fast you swing.

When the ball is lying down in the

Around the green, with a good lie, stand open, your weight towards the left. Swing smoothly and the ball will come out high and land softly.

Having a Rough Time

rough, short or long, you must play the ball well back in your stance, keeping the hands ahead of the club face. This has the effect of de-lofting the club so the ball will come out lower than for the floater, and run on landing. In severe instances the ball can be played in line with the right foot (providing the feet are about twelve inches apart), which will help to guarantee a descending strike.

The swing is made by cocking the right hand and wrist, which effectively means you "pick the club up" on the backswing rather than using the normal long, low take-away, then hitting down on the ball. To increase the length of the shot swing the arms back further.

The mistake most often made with this shot is that, in trying to be too delicate, the player quits on the shot completely, in effect decelerating the club before it reaches the ball. Have a practice swing, trying to determine the strength of shot required, being sure to swing through the grass.

Remember, it is better to get the ball somewhere on the green than to leave it in the rough, so do not try to be too clever and attempt the impossible. The one vital thing to remember in all these situations, as in a bunker, is to get the ball back in play first time, every time. Only as you become more proficient at golf, through practice, will you be able to get the ball to land almost exactly where you want it.

With the ball nearly buried close to the green, have the ball well back in your stance and hit down on it – don't try to hit it up. Punch down on it.

On the Green

You only score when the ball goes in the hole.

On the Green

Putting is almost a seperate game on its own for, however good your driving, long game and approach shots, if you can't putt, you won't score well.

With an average par of 72 for most golf courses, half those shots – 36 – should, if the rest of your game is good, be with the putter. Very few people spend half their practice time putting!

Putting is often regarded as a very personal skill, with a variety of different grips and styles. Some people stand fairly upright; some, like Jack Nicklaus, are almost bent double over the ball; some have a fairly straightforward grip; others, like Bernhard Langer, grip the putter with one hand and the left arm with the other. Some players, like Sam Torrance, use the "broom-handle" putter, resting it under their chin.

Is there, however, a right way – one that will guarantee success?

The answer has to be, sadly, no. If there was, every professional player in the world would be putting the same way and holing out every time. There are though, several things you can do to give yourself a better chance of holing both the long and the short putts.

The first essential ingredient to good putting is to find a good putter. That may sound so basic as to be silly but you would be amazed at the number of amateur golfers who are not comfortable with their putters.

Fortunately, putters don't come as part of sets of golf clubs so you choose them individually. You can also normally try them out in a golf shop or on the putting green at a golf club. Trying putters won't damage them as it would other clubs as you don't have to

Good putt – Seve sinks another one.

hit the ball a hundred yards.

Putters vary in length as well as style. Even if the shaft needs shortening, be sure that yours does not stick into your stomach at address.

Heel and toe weighted putters are by far the most popular, since they have a bigger sweet spot than a blade putter.

Go to the pro shop at the golf club and try a few out – don't buy the first one you see because it looks nice. Be happy with the weight of the putter.

On, then, to the task of putting.

As with all other shots in golf there are some fundamentals which are essential if you are to strike the ball well and on target.

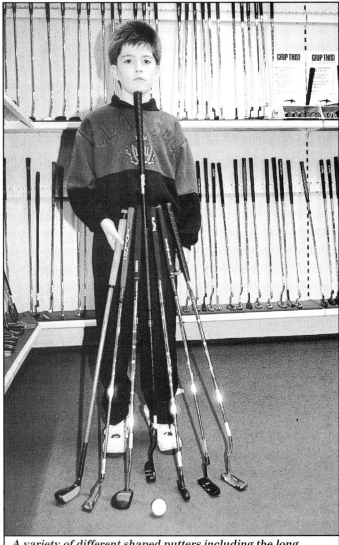

A variety of different shaped putters including the long 'broomhandle' style used by Sam Torrance.

Reverse overlap grip

Most good putters use this grip, which helps to firm up the back of the left wrist as you don't want to be too "wristy" when putting – the left wrist in particular should stay firm throughout the putting stroke.

To adopt this grip, place both hands completely on the grip, with the thumbs at the front, and the palms at right angles to the target line. Then lift up the left forefinger, slide the hands together, and place the forefinger over the fingers of the right hand. This may seem strange to start with, but persevere as it will definitely improve your putting.

On the Green

Address

Place the putter head square to the target (not necessarily the hole), then align your shoulders parallel to the target. Feet can be open, square, or closed, but shoulders MUST be square. You should angle forward from the hips, so that your arms can swing freely, and position the ball under your left eye. To check this, drop a second ball from under this eye; it should hit the one on the ground.

Weight usually remains fairly even, but in putting there is more leeway for some individuality, so you may prefer to put a little more on the front foot just to anchor yourself. The width of stance is also variable, so find one that feels comfortable. Faldo has a very wide stance, whilst American Ryder Cup player Chip Beck putts with his feet almost together. Try various widths of stance until you get the one which feels comfortable for you. You will probably find that one with your feet reasonably close together will be best, unless you are putting in a very strong wind when a wider stance will help you maintain better balance.

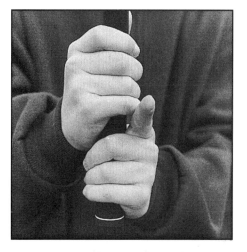

The hands should be just ahead of the ball, so that the shaft slopes slightly towards the target.

Many putter heads have a little white mark on the top to actually help you with your alignment. This is perfectly legal. Place the putter behind

Place your hands on the putter (top). Remove the first finger of the left hand and slide your hands together (centre). Overlap the right hand with the left forefinger (bottom).

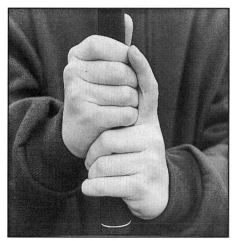

the ball, with the ball opposite this mark, which should point at your target. It may also help you to have an intermediate target, such as a small blemish on the green about a foot ahead of the ball, over which to aim.

The Stroke

The best putters in golf use a very firm wristed stroke, so that the putter is moved mainly by the arms. If you watch Faldo you would get the impression that the shoulders are the prime movers, but they are not. They simply move because the arms are moving; the triangle of the arms and shoulders remains intact throughout the stroke.

Most poor putters let the back of the left wrist collapse at impact. The reverse overlap grip helps to prevent this, but be sure to keep the back of

the left wrist moving throughout. This type of stroke will keep the putter head low to the ground. You should be bringing the putter slightly inside the line on the backswing, particularly on longer putts. Try to make the putter head go towards the hole as you swing through.

Success comes from striking the ball in such a way that, as you follow through, the back of your left hand moves towards the hole, pointing at it as you finish the stroke. The putter head should also finish pointing along the line of the putt.

The body and head remain very still; do not be too eager to see where the ball has gone; keep your eyes glued to the ground, and guess where the ball has gone, (no cheating). It is often said that on a short putt you should hear the ball drop in the hole, not see it.

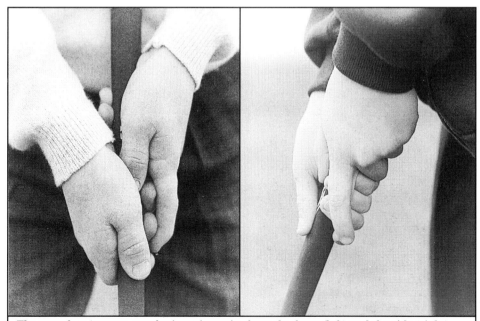

The complete 'reverse overlap' putting grip, from the front (left) and the side (right).

On the Green

Because of the set-up, the ball is struck when the club is at the base of its arc or just on the way up. If you hit down on the ball it will jump and might then bobble across the green, missing its target.

Try to imagine that you are rolling the ball across the green, as in ten-pin bowling, rather than throwing it. This will keep the stroke smooth, and help to keep the putter on line. Positioning the maker's name on the ball so that it points along the target line also helps to give you the picture of rolling the ball (and the name) over and over.

To experience the feeling of the correct action without a putter, take your address position, but with your palms together, fingers pointing to

Putting Drill.

the ground. Now just move your arms and hands back and through, and you will feel how they work as a unit, with no independent action by the wrists.

How far should you swing back?

That depends solely on the length of the putt and the speed of the green. What you should be looking to do is to swing the club back as far as you swing it through, just like a pendulum.

Many bad putts are hit because of either too short or too long a backswing. If it is too short, there is the

Pendulum putting.

temptation to "hit" at the ball with the hands, instead of rolling it. Usually, in such cases the ball is turned very much off line. With too long a backswing, the putter head is decelerating and the strike is not positive enough. Always try to imagine how far you would take your arm back if you were to hold the ball and roll it across the green.

To start with the beginner may find it easier to imagine putting into an area the size of a dustbin lid around the hole. This is a simpler task because it is a bigger target. Once you become fairly confident of doing that, always imagine holing each putt, really try to "see" the ball dropping into the hole before you putt.

How do you line up a putt?

Crouch a few feet behind the ball and look carefully along the intended line of the putt towards the hole. Look at the ground one yard either side of the hole. Is it higher one side than the other? If so the ball will turn towards the low side at the hole, so you must aim to the high side accordingly. If you play a hilly course, but feel that the green is flat, the chances are you are wrong. On most hilly courses the green slopes the way of the surrounding land. The amount of borrow will also depend on how hard you hit the putt. The slower a ball rolls the more borrow it will take.

One thing you will often see the tour players doing is to "plumb" a putt – holding the putter up and looking along the line between the ball and the hole.

The way to do this is to crouch down several feet behind the ball, close one eye with the putter shaft covering the ball. If the green is flat you won't be able to see the hole, which will be covered by the putter shaft as well. If you can see the hole on the left of the shaft the ball needs to be hit slightly to the right; if the hole can be seen on the right it should be aimed slightly left.

Putting perfection can only be achieved through constant practice. Remember, it is the speed of the putt which is more important than having it precisely on line. Get it close on the long putts and the short ones become simple.

Practising on the putting green can be great fun. Try holing three balls from one foot away; then go two feet away and hole those; then three feet and so on. It will improve your putting no end.

Inside path and low to the ground.

Eyes over ball and target line.

Follow through on line.

On the Green

How to Mark the ball on the green

On the green you are allowed to lift the ball and clean it, often to take it out of the way of another player's putt but you must mark the spot where the ball has been. You can use either a small coin or a ready-made ball marker, either buying them from the pro shop or using those which are attached to some makes of golf glove.

The way to mark is to carefully place the marker behind the ball. When you replace the ball you put the ball down in front of the marker, in the same position it was and then take away the marker.

Sometimes your marker may be on the line of another putt and your playing partner might ask you to move it. Put your marker down first, find a landmark off the green to line up (it might be a tree or a post), then place the putter head directly between your marker and the line of that landmark. Move the marker. If you can't find a suitable landmark use a tee-peg, sticking it into the ground on the edge of the green, and line up on that.

When you are to replace the ball make sure you move the marker back to its original position before replacing the ball in front of it. Never move the ball before marking.

Pitch Mark Repair

Before we leave the green, just a very brief word on pitch marks and how to repair them. When you walk on to a green always repair your pitch mark and two or three others – sadly, not every one does so you will normally see a few that other golfers have selfishly left unrepaired.

Contrary to what many people believe you should not repair a pitch mark by lifting the damaged soil upwards – that will only leave a mark on the green. You push soil into the gap from the outsides of the indentation, then just gently tap down with the putter head to flatten the surface.

It's no fun putting on a green covered in pitch marks. Be a caring golfer.

Marking and moving marker – always behind the ball.

On the Green

Practice on the Green

Two good practice routines to improve your putting. On the right, lay two clubs down parallel to one another and practice putting between them. This helps you keep the putter straight and on line. Then place balls around the hole, about two feet away. Hole each one. Then move them another six inches away and try from there, until you are regularly holing all of them from ten feet or more.

The Rules of Golf

A good knowledge of the rules of golf is essential – professionals have referees available on the course – you don't.

The Rules of Golf

Every game has rules – golf is no exception. Understanding them will help your game and save you wasting shots. Many rules are written in that dry, semi-legal way that is often difficult to fully understand, yet if you can read them, and understand them, they could help you in your golf. If you don't understand anything, ask the professional at your local golf club – he really won't mind helping you.

There are, also, local rules on every course – these are found on the scorecard and must be understood as they vary from course to course.

What we have done here in this section is to take a few of the most common instances and show you exactly what to do.

On the Tee

Even before you start you should check that you have no more than fourteen clubs, including the putter.

The teeing ground is marked and you are not allowed to play from in front of the markers. You can, however, play anything up to two club lengths behind the markers.

You don't have to stand inside the markers – only the ball needs to be in the imaginary square.

On the first tee the player with the lowest handicap normally plays first. On the second and subsequent tees the winner of the previous hole has the "honour" of playing first.

Read the Rules of Golf and the local rules which appear on the scorecard for each course.

The Rules of Golf

Obstructions and Impediments

One of the biggest problems encountered by golfers is deciding what an obstruction really is and what counts as an impediment.

If your drive has strayed a little off line and you find yourself behind a tree, for example, you normally have to play the ball as it is. There is one exception though.

If the tree is staked – usually young trees are staked to help them stay upright as they grow – and it or any support interferes with your stance or your swing, you have a free drop as it is defined (by the club under the local rule 24-2b (i) on the card) as an immovable obstruction.

This allows you to, first, find your nearest point of relief – that is the nearest point from where you can play the ball without the tree or its supports interfering with your stance or swing, BUT NOT NEARER THE HOLE – mark it with a tee peg.

Then using the longest club in the bag, usually the driver, measure one club length from that point and mark it with another tee peg. This is the extent of the area in which you may quite legitimately drop the ball, even if it is on the fairway, and the ball had been in the rough (unless the local rules forbid this).

Mark the ball with a tee peg, then lift it from its original position (you may clean it if you wish); then standing so that the ball will drop into the measured area drop the ball from shoulder height.

If it finishes within two club-lengths of where it first struck the

With the ball near a staked tree (1) you are allowed a free drop. First find the nearest point of relief (2), measure one club-length (3), and then you can drop the ball. It must not roll more than two club-lengths from where it first strikes the ground.

ground, that's fine – you play it from there, without adding any penalty stroke.

If it rolls more than two club-lengths away from the point where it hits the ground, drop it again. If it rolls away a second time place it where it hit the ground when you dropped it the second time, or very close to it. Again, you incur no penalty.

What other immovable obstructions are there on a golf course?

Telegraph poles, electricity pylons, a greenkeeper's hut, or anything else made by man and firmly fixed to the ground are immovable obstructions and you are entitled to relief from them if your stance or swing are impaired. Sprinkler heads, too, are immovable obstructions. Always read the course card, because that may list other immovable obstructions.

Movable obstructions can, as the term implies, be moved. They could include benches, lawn-mowers, rakes, hoses, or anything else you can move without breaking your back. If the ball moves whilst you are moving the obstruction you can replace it without penalty.

Loose impediments are natural objects, such as twigs, leaves, stones and fir-cones.

Loose impediments can be moved, with one exception. If you are in a hazard, such as a bunker or within the boundary of a water-hazard, you can not move any loose impediments. This means that stones in a bunker cannot be moved unless the local rules permit it. More and more clubs these days have such a local rule, thus

A movable obstruction. This stake and rope can be moved – but you should replace them after your shot.

An immovable obstruction. Most paths count as immovable and you are allowed a free drop. Check the local rules though.

saving you damaging your sand wedge or even your eyes, but do check the local rules first.

Twigs and leaves in bunkers or other hazards cannot be moved. However, discarded rubbish, like drink cans and cigarette packets, can – these were put there by thoughtless man, not nature.

A rake in or near a bunker can be moved – if your ball moves whilst you are removing it, you replace the ball where it was. Rakes should normally be left in a bunker, not on the edge.

Whilst still in the bunker, never ground your club before playing the shot – that incurs a penalty. If you hit the sand on your take-away that counts as grounding the club – two strokes in strokeplay, loss of hole in matchplay.

Twigs and leaves in a bunker can NOT be moved.

Loose impediments . Twigs and leaves on the fairway CAN be moved.

Some items can be moved in a bunker; this rake, for example, can be moved.

The Rules of Golf

Be very careful when moving loose impediments anywhere on the course, for if your ball moves you incur a one-stroke penalty, and you must replace the ball on its original spot.

Roads and paths are normally obstructions (though check the local rules) and you can have a free drop if your ball is either on them or you have to stand on them to play the shot. The path behind the 17th at St Andrews is one good example of a road that is part of the course and not an obstruction. If you land on that you have to play the ball as it is.

Out of Bounds (Rule 27)

Every course has boundaries round the edges. They are clearly marked with white posts or boundary walls and fences. There may also be some out-of-bounds areas within the course itself. These will be listed in the local rules you normally find on the score-card.

If you hit a ball out of bounds you have to replay the shot from the same place as the original one, adding an extra penalty stroke. Thus, if you hit a tee-shot out of bounds you replay from the tee, now hitting your third shot.

You cannot play a ball from an area out of bounds, though if you can see it by all means pick it up and keep it – golf balls are not cheap!

Ground Repair (Rule 25-1)

Ground under repair is usually clearly marked with a sign with the letters "G.U.R.", or by a white line around the area. If your ball lies in this area, or you have to stand in it, you MAY take relief. Some clubs prohibit play from this area, and you must take relief. After marking it, lift the ball and drop it within one club length of the nearest point of relief outside the ground under repair, but

Water hazard – a stream crossing the fairway, for example.

not nearer the hole. The dropping procedure is exactly the same as that described for staked trees.

Water Hazards (Rule 26)

These fall into two categories – water hazards and lateral water hazards – and they are treated differently so learn which is which. You should also realise that a water hazard need not necessarily contain water; it could be a dried-up pond or ditch, for example. The boundaries are normally marked by either yellow posts – water hazard – or red posts – lateral water hazard. Draw an imaginary line between these to establish whether you are in a water hazard or not.

Although you can play from inside a water hazard you can not ground your club in it, the same as in a bunker. Grounding the club incurs a two-stroke penalty.

If your ball is either lost or unplayable in a water hazard, you play another one, having dropped it; the place you drop it varies depending on whether it is a water hazard or a lateral water hazard.

Water hazards normally cross the fairway, from one side to another. Lateral water hazards

run in the same direction as the hole.

If the ball is in a water hazard you have three options: (A) You can drop the ball as far back as you like keeping the point where the ball last crossed the boundary of the hazard between you and the hole; (B) you can go back to the place where you last played and play another shot; or (C) you can play the original ball as it lies. You add one penalty stroke for each of the first two.

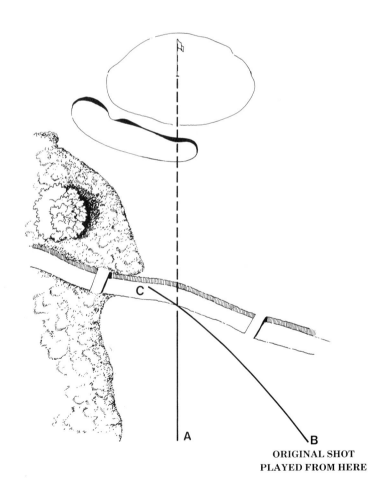

ORIGINAL SHOT
PLAYED FROM HERE

Water hazard – where to drop

The Rules of Golf

Lateral water hazard.

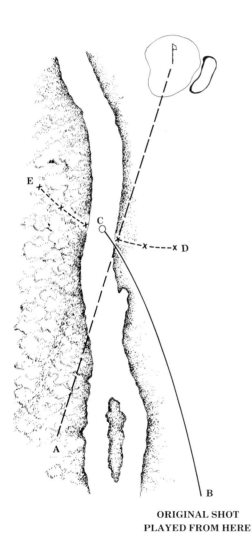

ORIGINAL SHOT
PLAYED FROM HERE

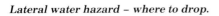

Lateral water hazard – where to drop.

For a lateral water hazard you have five options. You can do A, B or C as illustrated (with the penalty stroke unless you play it as it lies); you can also drop another ball within two club-lengths of the spot where the ball last crossed the hazard (D); or you can go to the other side of the hazard and drop within two club lengths' of that spot – again no nearer the hole (E). In each case you incur a penalty-stroke.

Casual Water

Casual water normally occurs in winter when a small part of the course may be temporarily flooded – in a little dip, perhaps, or quite often in a bunker.

You can lift and drop away from the

casual water – again, not nearer the hole – without penalty, if either your ball is in the casual water or you have to stand in it to make a stroke. As with other relief situations, you find your nearest point of relief then mark one club length from that before dropping. The ball must not roll more than two club-lengths from where it lands, and not nearer the hole.

If the casual water is in a bunker you must drop the ball in the same bunker – you can't drop it outside, unless you add a penalty shot by declaring the ball unplayable, in which case you go back to the point from which you played the previous shot, or drop it outside the hazard, keeping the point where the ball was directly between you and the hole. In both cases you add a penalty shot plus the shot you are now taking.

Divot Marks and Animal Scrapings

You can obtain relief from animal scrapings and burrowings but not from divot marks. If your ball disappears down a rabbit hole in the middle of the fairway, you can place another ball at your nearest point of relief (not nearer the hole – the one on the green!) without penalty.

On the Green

Once on the green you are entitled to relief if casual water, GUR, or sprinkler heads get in your way or are on the line of your putt. Here, you can lift and place (never drop) the ball, but not nearer the hole.

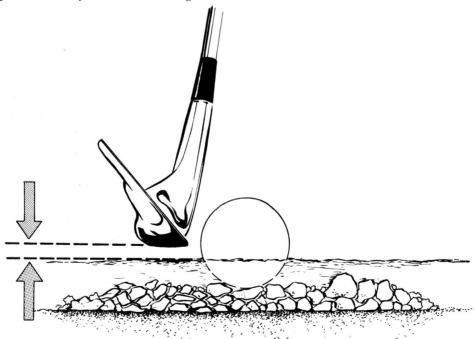

Playing from a water hazard – don't ground club.

The Rules of Golf

On the green you are also allowed to move twigs, stones, sand, leaves or other natural objects on the line of your putt, and repair any pitch marks or animal scrapes. Strangely, you are not allowed to repair spike marks made by other golfers' (or your own) shoes. However, if you have accidentally scraped your spikes on the green, AFTER you have completed the hole please do tap them back down.

On the green you can lift and clean your ball but make sure you mark it in the correct fashion – see page 90.

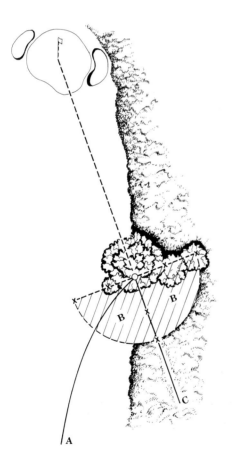

Unplayable – where to play options.

The player furthest from the hole normally putts first. You must also decide whether you want the flag left in, tended or taken out. If your putt hits the flag-stick you incur a one-stroke penalty, so either have it taken out (and put down OFF the green) or have it tended. The only exception to this is if you are putting from off the green – if you hit it then, that's o.k.

It is polite to hold the flag itself if it's windy so as not to distract the player putting. Also, never stand with your shadow across the hole.

Lost Ball

If you are unfortunate enough to lose your ball you play another from the point where you played the last, adding a penalty stroke. That might mean a long walk back to the tee, so most people, if they see their ball heading towards an area where it might be lost, play a provisional ball.

Then, go and look for the first one, remembering to call through any players behind you. You are allowed five minutes to look for a ball, no more. If you find the first one, play it as it lies, pick up the second ball; no penalty strokes are incurred.

If you don't find it within the five minutes, play the second from where it lands and add a penalty stroke.

Unplayable Ball

If you find your ball but consider it impossible to play (in the middle of a bush, or tree for example), you declare

When the ball is unplayable consider your options carefully.

it unplayable. You have three options:

A. Go back to the place from which you played the last shot, adding one penalty stroke – called stroke and distance.

B. Drop it within two club-lengths of the spot where it now is, but not nearer the hole, adding one penalty stroke.

C. Drop back as far as you like, keeping the spot where the ball lay between you and the hole, adding one penalty shot.

Although there are other rules in golf these are the ones most commonly encountered.

Whenever you come up against a situation about which you are unsure, always be certain to ask the club professional when you get back to the pro shop or club-house. It is rare for golfers to know all the rules of golf. Learn as many as you can – it will benefit you greatly.

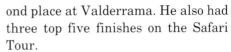

Pro Quote

Steve Richardson

Steve Richardson, born the son of a St Andrews professional but brought up in Hampshire, burst onto the European scene in 1991 with dramatic wins in Gerona and Portugal which helped him achieve a Ryder Cup place in 1991, only his second year on the Tour. In his first year he had won £110,000, including a fine joint sec-

ond place at Valderrama. He also had three top five finishes on the Safari Tour.

Getting there was, though, not without much hard work and Steve was a top junior and young player, winning the English Amateur Championship in 1989. That prompted him to turn professional and he came 36th in the PGA European Tour Qualifying School before setting out on a very successful career.

"It is important to start young," he says, "about 8 or 9 being the ideal age because by then you have enough strength to swing a club properly.

"The other important thing to do is to spend a lot of time practising, even when your friends are going off to play round the local course – or perhaps playing football.

"If you can practise whilst they are playing you will learn far more about the game, providing you practise properly and with a definite purpose.

"The last point I would make is to keep what natural abilities you have. Learn the correct grip, stance and positioning, but don't get too technical. Keep your natural abilities. To parents and professional coaches I would say, don't over-coach youngsters, teach them the basics that everyone must get right but leave them with their natural style and talent."

Never play unless it is safe to do so.

Etiquette

The way you behave on a golf course says a lot about your character. There are, sadly, a few people who, on missing a simple putt or mis-hitting a shot, get angry and throw their club. This can be extremely dangerous as well as damaging to the club and your reputation.

There really is no excuse for club-throwing tantrums in golf and any player stooping to such a level would be regarded with some disdain by other golfers. After all, we all miss an easy shot sometimes!

Golf is often referred to as an inner game, one great teacher of the past having said that the most important six inches in golf is the space between the ears. Certainly, if something goes wrong you only have yourself to blame, for you are totally in control of the shot, the ball being still before you hit it, unlike tennis or football where you might get a bad bounce.

Tantrums are, thankfully, few and far between yet there are other points

Don't swing near other players – it could be disastrous.

of etiquette of which you should be aware.

The first is to remain still and quiet when someone near you is playing the ball – it might not even be in your group but on a nearby tee, green or fairway which you are passing. Quite often a tee is close to the previous green and those putting should allow the players in front to tee off in silence – players in front normally have priority.

The same goes if two fairways cross, as they occasionally do. The players further on in their game have right of way.

The second point to understand is

that, if you lose your ball in the thick rough and have to search for it, you are allowed five minutes under the Rules of Golf to find it. You should, though, call the following group through to save them waiting. Have a quick look, by all means, but if you haven't found it in about thirty seconds, be courteous and call them through whilst you continue looking.

You must never play until the players in front are out of range – this may seem obvious, for a golf ball can injure or even kill someone, yet some inexperienced golfers do play, thinking they will not reach, but then hit the shot of their lifetime, nearly decapitating the players in front.

The rule is simple – wait until the players in front are well out of reach.

Don't, though, hold others up by slow play. Be ready to play when it's your turn, rather than standing next to your opponent or partner and watching him play, before going to your own ball.

When your partner or opponent is playing, however, don't stand in front of them; you should never stand closer to the green than anyone in your group when they are playing a shot. Be careful where you take a practice swing, check no one is

Always replace a divot, carefully treading it down.

close. Equally, keep well away from players who are practice swinging as they may not hear you approaching. Never swing towards anyone, you may inadvertently hit a stone and injure them.

Always replace divots by picking up the divot, placing it back in the ground and stamping it gently in round the edges. That helps it to take root again and will keep the course in good condition.

Before leaving a bunker always rake it, smoothing over any marks you have made. If there is no rake available, use your feet and the club to smooth over the sand.

On the green always repair pitch marks – a good idea is to repair yours and three others.

Another point on the green concerns the flagstick. You should not drop it but place it just off the edge of the green where it will not damage the putting surface. Golf carts and trolleys should, of course, not be taken onto the green at all.

Finally, rubbish! No, not the way we play golf but the bits of discarded rubbish sometimes seen blowing around a golf course. Put all your own litter – empty drink cans, snack wrappers and so on – in a rubbish bin. If there isn't one near, put it in your golf bag and empty it at the nearest bin. You wouldn't drop rubbish in the lounge at home – don't do it on the golf course!

Golf is a game to be enjoyed – by everyone, most of all, you. If the course is in good condition you will have a better game.

Tending the flag-stick. Hold the flag itself to stop it flapping about in the wind. Don't let your shadow fall across the hole.

Course Strategy

Plan carefully before you hit the ball.

Course Strategy

Playing a golf course is not just a matter of hitting the ball as far as possible, though in many cases distance is important. That distance will only be built up over time but in the meantime you can score better by carefully planning your way round a golf course.

Generally speaking, once you have learnt to hit the ball, you must learn where to hit it. This may sound obvious but often requires strict discipline to plot your route. It is impossible to copy the world stars if you cannot hit the ball like them (yet).

So you must learn to use your head and to have a plan for each hole.

Every hole is measured, the distance appearing on the score-card and on a marker on the tee. The important things to look for are the par values (3, 4, or 5), and the stroke-index (S.I.), which tells you how difficult the hole is to play, relative to the other holes on the course. S.I. 1 is the hardest hole, and S.I. 18 the easiest.

So let us imagine that you are an 18 handicap player. This means your par values are 4, 5, and 6, and you should plan your play so that on the par 3s you are on the green in no worse than two shots, (many players, even the beginners will be on the very short holes in 1), on the green at the par 4s in three, and the par 5s in four shots. In some cases you will beat these targets, but use them as a realistic guide and you will take away a lot of pressure. On each hole you then have two putts to achieve your own personal "par".

So on each tee, try to have a plan of how you would like to play the hole, in order to be on the green in the correct number of shots.

Generally speaking if you stay out of the hazards, both watery and sandy, you will score better, so have that uppermost in your game plan.

Do not always use a wood off the tee if this means you are likely to reach a ditch or bunker. Perhaps hit an iron and lay up short. The same strategy is correct for the second shot, keep out of the hazards.

Beware that the pin does not become too much of a magnet. From perhaps 100 yards out, play for the centre of the green until you are proficient enough to be more accurate. If the hole is cut to one side of the green quite close to a bunker, and you aim at the pin, you will not have to be too far off target to hit the ball into the bunker. Play safe!

Once you are near the green, try to

Time: Competition:

Player:

| Marker | Hole | meters | | Par | Stroke | Player's result |
		Men	Ladies			
	1	456	440	5	15	
	2	314	302	4	11	
	3	390	325	4	5	
	4	383	318	4	3	
	5	204	164	3	13	
	6	416	366	4	1	
	7	446	429	5	7	
	8	130	123	3	17	
	9	339	299	4	9	
	Out	3078	2766	36		

Signatures: SSS 72

Marker:

Player:

Scorecard for S.I. and par.

imagine where you would like to putt from, but be realistic – I know 6 inches away would suit most people!

If the green is flat then you do not have to think too carefully, but on a sloping green always try to leave yourself with an uphill putt.

Beginners may find this beyond their capabilities to start with, but as a thinking process it will do you no harm. Remember golf is brain training as well as muscle training!

Golf is like a game of chess, always plan a move or two ahead, and you will improve.

The shape of the hole and the hazards plus your ability dictate strategy, so let us imagine how a professional would play a hole, then how you should tackle it.

The Professional

The professional would have no trouble carrying the ditch and, providing he did not draw the ball too much, would avoid the bunker.

For his second shot, although the pin is cut behind the bunker, his accuracy would allow him to aim at the pin.

The Club Golfer

Carrying the ditch requires that you hit perhaps one of your best shots, and this is added pressure. But remember this is not a par 4 for you, but a 5, so you only have to get onto the green in three shots. Choose a club that does not go as far as 170 yards, and tee up on the left of the tee, hitting towards the right half of the fairway.

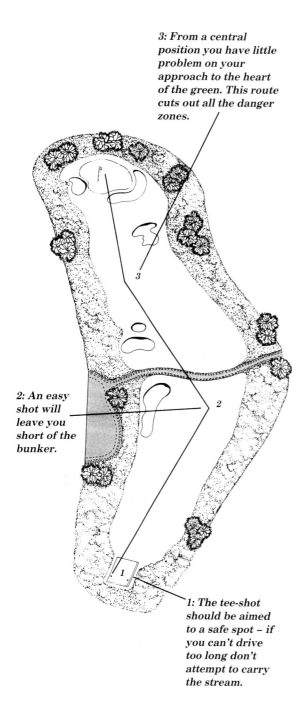

3: From a central position you have little problem on your approach to the heart of the green. This route cuts out all the danger zones.

2: An easy shot will leave you short of the bunker.

1: The tee-shot should be aimed to a safe spot – if you can't drive too long don't attempt to carry the stream.

Plan your way.

Course Strategy

This will leave you a second shot that does not have to carry the fairway bunker, and will allow you to aim to the left hand side of the fairway. From here you will not have to play over any bunkers even if you aim for the pin and not the centre of the green.

The importance of strategy is highlighted, for instead of trying to reach the green in two, which would have required a tee-shot of 220 yards and a second shot of 180 yards, both towards dangerous positions, you can now hit a tee-shot (perhaps with a 3- or 5-wood or long iron) about 160 yards to the wide part of the fairway, a second shot a further 130 yards to another safe position, and a short iron just over 100 yards to reach the safety of the green.

On The Green

Planning should not stop once you are on the green for by thinking a little you may save yourself from three putting or worse.

The beginner should try to achieve certainly no more than three putts, even from the edge of the green. For them, imagining a three-foot circle or a dustbin lid around the hole may be helpful. Better and more experienced players should aim to hole all putts. Once you start to believe you can do this, you may surprise yourself.

Flat greens do not present too many problems, but on sloping ones try to leave yourself an uphill putt if the first one does not go in.

On short sidehill putts, aim more

Plan your putts. With the flag at the back of the green, an over-hit putt could leave you in the semi-rough.

towards the high side than you think, then at least the ball has a chance of dropping in.

Professionals tend to hit the short putts with little break, firm and straight at the hole, so that the break does not affect the ball. This is okay if you are accurate, but if not you may have a longer putt from the other side of the hole coming back. Until you become proficient, aim to roll the ball so that it would only finish about one foot past if it misses.

Weather Conditions

Another major factor to take into account is the weather. You will often see top professionals picking up a blade of grass and throwing it into the air to see which way the wind is blowing, and how strong.

The wind does have a major impact on a golf ball, from whatever direction it is blowing.

Obviously, when it is blowing against you, the ball will not go so far and it is better to keep it low (see page 113). When the wind is behind you it will travel further. When there is a cross wind it will slow the ball down as well as pushing it to one side or the other, so pay careful attention to the wind direction and condition, not just on the tee but for every shot, including long putts.

Always look carefully at the flag and trees to determine wind speed and direction.

Course Strategy

How to play in wind

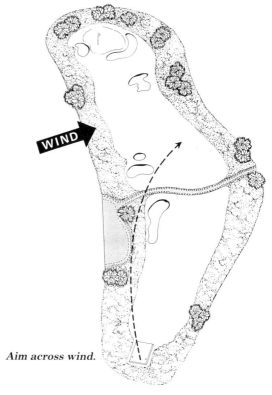

Aim across wind.

When the wind is against you the ball will travel less distance and will often have a different trajectory, travelling flatter to start with before climbing and then dropping almost vertically. If you are hitting to a green into the wind you can thus afford to hit extra club (but don't try to hit harder!) and the ball should drop onto the green and stop, rather than running on. If the distance is such that you would normally hit an 8-iron and the wind is very strong, you might need a 7-, or better still a 6-iron, gripping down the shaft. But don't try to hit it harder, just let the club do the extra work.

You will often find it more benefi-

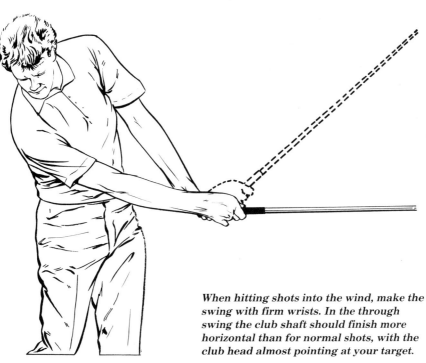

When hitting shots into the wind, make the swing with firm wrists. In the through swing the club shaft should finish more horizontal than for normal shots, with the club head almost pointing at your target.

cial, when playing into the wind, to keep the ball low where it is less affected by the wind than if hit high – wind strength increases the higher you go!

If, for example, you have an approach shot to the green where you would normally play a pitch shot, providing there are no bunkers in the way and the ground is reasonably flat, it could be more sensible to run the ball in low, using a 7-iron or something similar. Obviously, you would not hit the ball so hard and would have played it further back in your stance, effectively having de-lofted the club.

With the wind behind you the ball will travel greater distances, bouncing on once it lands. Whilst it is important not to land short, you should not over-hit a ball down-wind. When close to the green it is better, if the wind is behind you, to land the ball beyond the pin (providing this does not leave a vicious downhill putt) as it is easier to putt back into the wind than with it behind you.

On a cross wind, the ball will be blown accordingly, and will loose a little length, so you may need an extra club. Use the wind, do not fight it. Aim left or right of the target as necessary, and allow the wind to blow the ball back.

Practising in the wind can be

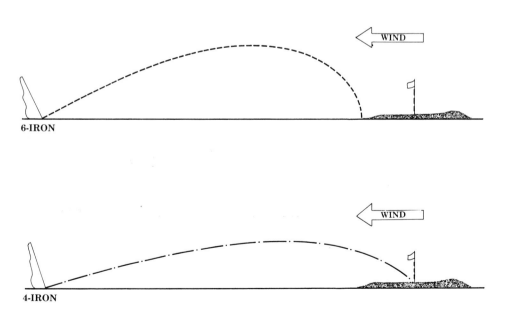

Into wind hit longer – the wind will hold the ball back. You will probably need to hit longer clubs.

Course Strategy

worthwhile and you will come to realise just how much the ball can be moved by the wind, and how far off to the left or right you need to aim. But never practice too long in the wind, especially a left to right, as you may develop bad faults and lose your rhythm. Ideally stand in a protected spot, so that you can keep your normal balance and never try to hit harder. Always remember what Tommy Armour, the Scots golfer who emigrated to the United States once said, "when it's breezy, swing it easy".

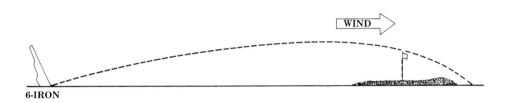

6-IRON

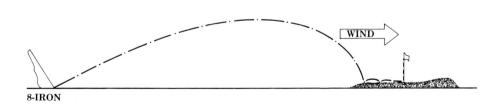

8-IRON

Wind behind – land the ball short of the target. The wind carries the ball further so use less club.

Course Strategy

Rain

In wet weather, the fairways can get a bit soggy and the ball will not run as it would on a dry fairway. You will thus get less distance. On the greens, too, the ball will "die" when it hits the green, not bouncing on as it would if the green was dry and hard. In the wet, and particularly in the winter, you can afford to "attack the pin", aiming the ball to land right by the flag, rather than short of it and run up.

Finding rainwear for younger golfers can be very difficult. Most are made for adults.

Course Strategy

Hitting off a wet fairway might also hinder your contact, so the ball needs to be hit "cleaner", sweeping it away rather than taking a big divot.

The most important thing in wet weather is to keep dry. Waterproof golfwear for younger golfers is expensive and often difficult to find, (try a camping shop maybe). Wear a waterproof golf glove, or keep a couple of extra gloves and one or two small towels in the golf bag, preferably in a plastic bag to ensure that they remain dry. Wipe the grips before each shot. Close your umbrella before putting it down – umbrellas often blow around in the wind.

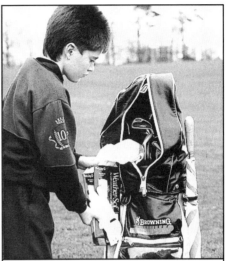

Always keep an extra couple of gloves in the bag when it's likely to rain.

An umbrella is an essential piece of golf equipment, even if you can't buy proper waterproofs.

Course Strategy

Uphill – Downhill

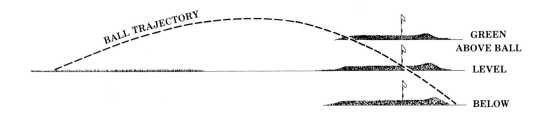

Height of green above and below ball and result.

If you are aiming at a green higher than you are, you will need more club as the trajectory of the ball would otherwise leave the ball short.

If hitting to a green lower than you, you need less club. If the distance is a six-iron, take a seven, or eight.

The 3rd at Woburn, a fine example of a green that is lower than the tee.

Course Strategy

Sloping Lies

You will not always be lucky enough to hit the ball from a flat and even lie, and certain adjustments to your set up and club selection must be made accordingly.

Uphill

Set up so that your spine is at right angles to the slope, with more weight on your right foot, the ball slightly nearer your left foot than normal. This set up will make your club more lofted, and will therefore send the ball higher than usual. So if you wish to hit the ball your normal 7-iron distance, you may need to hit the 6 or 5-iron. Try to swing the club along the slope of the ground. The ball is often pulled or hooked from this lie, so aim right a little to allow for it.

Downhill

Set up with your spine at right angles to the slope, which this time means putting more weight on your left foot. Position the ball further back in your stance, even back of centre on a very steep slope. This set up position takes loft off the club, and the ball flies lower than usual, so to hit the ball a 7-iron distance you may need to use an 8 or 9-iron. The ball is often pushed or faded from this lie, so aim left to allow for it. This is a more difficult lie than the uphill, and you must concentrate on swinging the club down the slope on the through swing, never try to hit the ball up into the air.

To help you remember these adjustments think as follows; Weight to the low foot, ball to the high.

119

Course Strategy

Sidehill Lies

Ball Below Feet

This shot is one of the least favourite of any golfer, but to play it successfully you need to make the changes mainly at the set up. Bend forward more from your hips, and increase the flex in your knees. Keep well balanced, with sufficient weight on your heels to stop you falling forward.

The swing is made by just swinging your arms up, do not try to turn your body too much. To get good contact, keep your eye on the ball, and then the grass it was sitting on, longer than usual.

Because of the upright swing the ball tends to fade, so aim left to allow for it. You will lose distance but be content to keep the ball in play, using no more than a 5-iron.

Ball Above The Feet

Of the four sloping lies this is the easiest to play. Do not bend forward so much from the hips, and play the ball centrally in your stance, gripping down the club on severe slopes. As your spine is more upright you will be able to turn more, and the club will be swung flatter. This produces a shot that tends to draw and to go further, so enjoy the shot!

With all shots from slopes, balance is most important, so swing within yourself, having one practice swing just to see how your balance is affected.

Course Strategy

Hitting The Ball High

You may need to hit the ball with extra height, perhaps to carry a tree. To play the shot successfully, you must have a good lie, so that there is a nice cushion of grass beneath the ball.

Set up the ball nearer your left foot than usual, open the club face a little, and aim slightly left of target.

Keep the hands level with the ball, and with a narrow stance, and just a little more weight on the right foot than the left, try to swing the club up, with an early wrist break.

This will create a steep out-to-in attack on the ball, and will send it higher than normal.

The set up will increase the loft on the club but do not be too ambitious, if you think a 7-iron will get you over, take the 8 to be sure.

Hitting The Ball Low

This is the shot to play into the wind, or to escape from under trees.

Play the ball back of centre in your stance, keeping your hands well ahead of the ball, and with a wider stance than normal keep a little more weight on the left side.

This set up takes loft off the club, providing that you keep the blade square, don't let it open at address.

The swing is shorter than normal, and very firm wristed. Punch the ball away, finishing with a three-quarter follow-through, wrists firm.

Practice will tell you how high or low the ball will go with different clubs, so experiment and become familiar with the high and low shots.

That is the mark of a true artist – a player who can make the ball do almost anything.

When you want to play pitch shots, don't just have the balls in a line – throw them around, giving yourself difficult shots. Make every shot different. Pitch or chip against a friend and see who can get the ball closest. Vary your bunker practice – have some at the front, some plugged, some with a downhill lie. Aim some at a nearby target, others at the far side of the green. Please rake the bunker after use.

Not all practice need be outside or at the golf course. You can help to improve your game by practising your address position indoors and checking it in a mirror. If there is room, see if the half way back position and top of the backswing look correct. Do be careful though, as you mustn't damage furniture or run the risk of hitting anyone.

Indoor putting on a smooth carpet is great practice. Try putting to a tee peg, then the hole will seem like a bucket!

You may be able to chip from a coconut mat onto your lawn. This will help to develop the stroke, and you can put down some targets to aim at, but preferably not the neighbour's greenhouse!

No practice session should be too long though, otherwise you will lose concentration – take a break now and then to refresh your mind and body.

Make it different, make it fun.

Practice Makes Perfect

If you want to be good at anything you must practise. Golf is no exception and the only way to improve your golf, having been taught what to do, is to go out and practise hard.

There must, though, be some purpose to it – it's pointless just going to a driving range and hitting ball after ball with little reason. Give some thought to what you are trying to learn before you begin. And make it fun!

First, find a good place to practise. Decide what you want to work on before you make up your mind where to go. If you want to improve your driving and long shots, a driving range might be ideal, though nothing compares to being able to hit shots off the grass.

If you want to chip and pitch, many golf clubs have areas where you can do this to a practice green. There is often a bunker here as well. For putting use only the putting green, although a smooth carpet at home can be ideal for winter putting practice.

Always warm up first, stretching your muscles and turning. A good exercise, which also helps you turn correctly, is to stand holding a club behind your back and turn both ways – into the backswing, then through to the finish, remembering to turn your body and bring the right leg through, as in the photograph sequence shown on page 32. It is also a good exercise to swing two clubs together – this builds up the back and shoulder muscles as well as helping you keep your rhythm slow and smooth.

Hit a few balls with an 8 or 9-iron first, just to get into the habit of swinging. Don't worry too much about these early shots. A visit to the practice range at any golf tournament will show you that the first shots from even top players are far from perfect. Only when they have warmed up will they be hitting the type of shots with which they are happy.

Find a good, safe place to practise, but always ensure you are not hitting towards any other golfers.

123

Practice Makes Perfect

Always have a target – a clearly definable, reachable target to aim at, even at a driving range.

Before you hit each shot go through the pre-shot routine – behind the ball, take the grip, align the club face, then the stance. Have a couple of practice swings too, to "feel" the shot.

Once you have hit what you believe is a good shot, repeat it until you can do it regularly. Try to hit your target six times running – that's adding mental pressure as well, something you have on the golf course.

If the shots are not working quite as you want check the basics:

● Grip
● Club face alignment
● Stance
● Ball position
● Posture.

Use clubs on the ground parallel to the target line to help with your alignment.

Warm up first.

Once these points are checked, concentrate on the swing path, balance and rhythm. It is very easy when practising to start to hit the ball too hard, so check that your swing remains smooth and you have the same rhythm for all the clubs. Never try to hit the ball too hard – hit smoothly.

Then try using different clubs to hit the same distance. There is one wonderful story of Ireland's Christy O'Connor playing a practice round at a tournament with a young professional. The rookie hit an 8-iron to the green of a par-3; O'Connor had taken a 6-iron.

A modern driving range – an ideal place to practise, particularly in winter.

Practice Makes Perfect

The young player suggested that it was only necessary to use an 8-iron and questioned why Christy had taken a 6-iron. O'Connor then proceeded to hit a ball with every club in the bag, from the driver to the pitching wedge. Every shot landed on the green.

That is the mark of a true artist – a player who could make the ball do almost anything.

When you want to play pitch shots, don't just have the balls in a line – throw them around, giving yourself difficult shots. Make every shot different. Pitch or chip against a friend and see who can get the ball closest. Vary your bunker practice – have some at the front, some plugged, some with a downhill lie. Aim some at a nearby target, others at the far side of the green. Please rake the bunker after use.

Not all practice need be outside or at the golf course. You can help to improve your game by practising your address position indoors and checking it in a mirror. If there is room, see if the half way back position and top of the backswing look correct. Do be careful though, as you mustn't damage furniture or run the risk of hitting anyone.

If you are having problems with your grip you can buy, or maybe borrow, a special club from your local professional. Known as a "training club" it has a specially-shaped grip which puts your hands in the correct position. It is impossible to hold the club properly unless your hands are set correctly.

Golfers need strong wrists and forearms. You can increase the strength of these by holding a squash or tennis ball in each hand and squeezing them in and out for ten minutes at a time.

It also helps, when on the practice area, to swing two clubs together, something that also slows down the speed of your swing and develops a good rhythm.

A visit to any golf tournament should include some time spent watching professionals practise. Their dedication to this is impressive.

Look and Learn

Whilst practising can help you enormously you will also find that watching other golfers – top professionals – will bring major benefits.

There are, these days, countless opportunities to watch the top players in action, either on television or at golf tournaments around the country. Television watching brings the extra bonus of often being able to watch a player's swing in slow motion, particularly if the commentator, as normally happens, analyses the swing.

When watching a golf tournament on television there are several points in particular to take note of. First, watch how carefully each player prepares for every shot, checking the exact distance with the help of his caddy, taking time in club selection, having regard to wind and weather conditions and, on an approach shot, the exact location of the pin.

On your local course you won't have the benefit of knowing the exact distance to the green, or to the pin for that matter, so you will have to make an intelligent guess.

Some courses have yardage guides showing the distance to the green from various points on the course – a tree, a fairway bunker or some other landmark. Whilst these are of use you should check whether these yardages are to the front of the green or its centre. Most greens are around thirty yards long, so the difference between hitting the front of the green and the back could be three clubs, each increase in club strength normally accounting for about ten yards.

It is important to get to know how far you hit each club and this you can do on the practice ground. Once you have warmed up hit six balls with each club, starting with a 9-iron and working up to a 3-wood or driver. Have specific targets in mind but don't try to hit the ball as hard as you possibly can. Swing normally and within your regular capabilities. What you are trying to do is to establish the **average** distance you hit each club.

Ideally, the six balls you hit with each club should land in a group. Ignore the longest and the shortest – there will always be one you hit poorly and also one you hit perfectly – and pace out the yardages to where most of the balls have landed.

You should find approximately ten yards difference between each club. As you improve and as your physical strength increases as you grow these distances will improve. An average man hits a 5-iron about 150-160 yards. A top professional player hits the same club about another forty yards.

If your course does not have a yardage chart go out one evening when the course is quiet and actually pace out various distances, just as the caddies on tour do. Make a note of the distances to the centre of the green from various landmarks then, when next you play, you will know that the distance to the middle of, say, the fifth green from the fairway bunker is 120 yards. Your practice ground work will tell you that perhaps your 6-iron will carry 120 yards and your club selection is made. It really is that simple.

You should, of course, take into account the wind conditions, as we discussed on pages 113 to 115, using a club less or a club more as required. Watching professionals on television will show you that they often throw a blade or two of grass into the air, to check the wind strength and direction carefully. You too will find this helpful.

One point we must stress here is that some top professionals often take far too long over their shots. You do not need to take so long. By all means think about your shot and what you want it to do – to fly high, to run in low, to fade or to draw – but don't stand there for ages just because you have seen Faldo or Ballesteros do it.

The time they take over a shot matches their skill – they can hit a ball to within a foot of their intended target (they don't always, of course); most average golfers would be pleased to get it within ten yards of the target.

Make up your mind what type of shot you wish to play and get on with it. Don't rush it, particularly if it is a difficult shot; nobody is suggesting you should just walk up to the ball and hit it, but don't be a tortoise!

The other advantage of television is the opportunity to watch top professionals swinging in slow motion. Every swing differs slightly, as some of the photographs in this section show, but note carefully that, even under pressure, every professional, on a full swing, completes the backswing fully, turning the shoulders so that the back is facing the target.

Getting to the completion of the backswing is important, but don't overdo it in an attempt to emulate John Daly, the long hitting winner of the 1991 USPGA tournament. Although the professionals complete the backswing they never lose their balance or control.

Watch carefully, too, how they keep their heads steady during the swing. There is no great up-and-down or side-to-side movement of the head until after impact. You will also see how they all swing through to a full, balanced finish, every time.

The finishing position at the end of the swing tells a great deal about the type of shot hit. Experienced commentators can, by looking at the finish, tell whether a shot is straight or has been pushed or pulled. Watch for the faults as well, making sure that, when you are out on the practice ground next, you don't finish in a poor position. Remember how the top players looked at the finish and try to copy them.

There are one or two players who take several practice swings before hitting the shot – José-Maria Olazabal is one; yet this is not really necessary. Take one by all means, but then get on with the shot. The only exceptions to this are where you have a difficult shot out of long grass, for instance, or when you are close to the green and need only a delicate little shot that must be hit just right.

On those occasions the professionals take a little longer, swinging the club a few times to "feel" the shot, gauging the length of backswing necessary to get the ball far enough but not too far. There is nothing wrong with you doing the same, but only if it helps you. Again, though, don't take too much time – you can be taking a

Look and Learn

Golf is played by people of all shapes and sizes and this obviously has a bearing on how the club is swung. Whilst golf teachers will endeavour to guide their pupils to incorporate sound principles into their swings, everyone swings differently.

The four players highlighted here have all been very successful, yet they all swing the club differently as we can see from the four different positions they achieve at the top of the backswing.

Lee Trevino's left wrist is very arched with a closed club face, the shaft pointing well left of target. He sets up with an open stance and generally fades the ball, although he is a master of shaping shots at will.

Fred Couples' left wrist looks to be almost cupped and his elbows have separated, causing the shaft to aim well right of the target. His arms and shoulders do not seem to work in unison on the backswing yet he develops enormous power, being one of the longest hitters in golf.

few practice swings whilst another player in your group is getting ready to play – but don't move if you are within his or her eye range as it can be distracting.

You might also have the opportunity to go to a golf tournament. Some, like the British Open, get very crowded but many others offer the opportunity to watch the top players in action without massive crowds.

Your first port of call at a tournament should be the practice ground; the earlier you get there, the better. Watch carefully how each player takes time to warm up, starting off their swing routine not with the driver, as do many club golfers when they get to a driving range, but with a 9-iron. They then work their way through the bag, hitting a number of balls with almost every club, normally finishing with the driver, until

Look and Learn

Nick Price gives the impression that his swing is short and sharp. His wrists have cocked in a more orthodox fashion but note how tightly his right elbow is clamped to the side of his body, producing a rather flat swing.

Ballesteros has a much more upright swing. His elbow is not clamped to his side like Nick Price. However, he has cocked his wrists so that the club face is parallel to the back of his left arm and is thus on the correct plane.

All four swing differently, yet they all get the club face back to the ball in a square position at impact, consistently. They all also get through to a good, balanced finish, hitting through the ball rather than at it. It is their consistency in reproducing the same swing every time which makes each of them a great player. Their pace and rhythm does not vary. Try to mimic them, with the more orthodox swing (such as Faldo or Ballesteros) being the one to copy, yet keep in mind that there is a place in golf for individual style and flair.

they are happy that they are swinging smoothly for that day.

Note how they often help one another, or take advice from coaches, caddies or other players – none of them are afraid to ask for help, or to listen when another player has a comment or suggestion to make. Golf is a game where we cannot watch ourselves – but others can watch us. On your local course take note of what more experienced players, or the club professional, might have to say about your swing. Try to watch your friends when they are swinging to see if you can pick out any good points, or any faults. Seeing faults in others helps you to understand what you should avoid.

You may often see players laying a club on the ground to help them line up to their target. This is something we suggested earlier in this book.

Look and Learn

Never be afraid to do it on the practice ground.

Watch, too, how their rhythm stays the same for every shot, from the driver to the wedge. You don't swing any faster with a driver; it's the same pace of swing for every club – only the length of the backswing varies. The top players use no more effort hitting a driver 300 yards than they do hitting a wedge 100 yards.

Although not all golf clubs have good practice facilities, if you do have the chance to practise for thirty minutes before you play you will definitely feel the benefit.

From the practice ground you will want to spend part of the day out on the course watching the players. You can either choose one vantage point and watch how a number of players swing, or you can follow one group around, going from tee to green. Again, note how they line up their shots, how they complete the backswing and how they finish. It is also interesting to watch how they get out of trouble when they have hit a wayward shot. They don't rush, they don't panic. They think about the shot, weighing up all their options and choosing the achievable shot they know they can hit, rather than the one-in-a-hundred shot of a lifetime.

None of them hit shots they think are beyond their capabilities. Be the same – never try to play a shot you are unsure about.

Before we take a closer look at the swing sequences of a few players, a word about golf balls. At any tournament, whether you are there or watching at home on television, you will see countless shots to the green landing beyond the pin and then spinning back. Every amateur player tries to learn the secret of this, believing, falsely, that it is something they should all do.

To start with, very few club golfers hit the ball past the pin anyway. To get a golf ball to spin back it needs to be hit with backspin. Professionals normally use balata golf balls. These have a soft cover which allows the ball to be hit with more backspin, providing perfect contact is made between club and ball. Few average golfers can achieve this with any degree of regularity.

A balata ball spins faster; if it is hit straight it will spin back on landing. If it is not hit perfectly any hint of a slice or hook will be exaggerated, causing it to veer off course even more.

Balata balls also cut more easily, because they have soft covers. During a tournament professionals will change their golf ball every three or four holes, more often if they have been in bunkers. Because they are so easily damaged balata balls are not a sensible option for the average golfer.

There are two other main types of ball – surlyn wound and solid two-piece.

For the beginner and shorter hitter the solid two-piece ball is ideal. It spins less rapidly, thus staying on line better; it is very durable, being almost un-cuttable; and it will give more distance on most shots. It is, though, not so controllable on the green, tending to run on landing rather than stopping fairly quickly.

Look and Learn

Lanny Wadkins, one of the world's great golfers, has strayed from the straight and narrow and found himself in deep rough. All he can do from this position is to get back on the fairway first time, without wasting any more shots.

As most golfers tend to be short of the pin anyway, this need not be a problem and this type of ball could be ideal to begin with.

As your skill improves the surlyn wound ball provides more control, though still giving good distance and durability. In the summer particularly, when the greens are hard, the surlyn wound ball is better for it is easier to control on the greens.

Most ball manufacturers make all three types of ball; which you use is a matter of personal choice.

When you are on the practice ground try to use balls that are not cut or severely damaged as they do not fly as well as new balls.

Look and Learn

Sandy Lyle

Many hours of practice enabled Sandy to produce one of the most famous shots in golf when he played from a fairway bunker on the 18th at Augusta to the heart of the green on his way to winning the 1988 Masters Tournament.

Here he is hitting a cut shot from the bunker, having set up open to the target, as indicated by the line he has drawn in the sand. Of course you can only do this when practising – not in a round of golf!

At the top of his swing you can see that the shaft is parallel to his shoulder line at address. This will create a steep out-to-in attack on the ball, ensuring that he contacts the ball first, not the sand. This is for a fairway bunker shot, where distance is vital. Don't forget that for a short bunker shot you will be hitting the sand first.

Look and Learn

You can see quite clearly how the club is approaching the ball from outside the target line. Sandy is transferring his weight onto his left side, but in a smooth manner.

As with a normal shot from the fairway the follow through has been completed with the weight now fully on the left side, the right heel having turned and lifted. He is, though, perfectly balanced at the finish.

The key to successful long bunker shots is to select the right club and then to keep the swing smooth, contacting the ball first and not the sand.

Severiano Ballesteros

(1) *No player in golf looks better than Ballesteros at address. He sets up with his spine angled well forward, creating plenty of space in which to swing in his graceful, but powerful manner. His legs are comfortably flexed; note particularly how much space there is between his hands and his legs. His head is up, yet his eyes are looking down at the ball.*

(2) *With his hands almost at waist height the club face is square and his shoulders have already begun to turn. He has not made as much movement with his hips as some players, yet he is a very athletic golfer.*

(3) *At the top of the backswing the right leg has retained its address position and is now taking most of his weight. Seve's shoulders have turned at least 90 degrees but his hips have still not turned fully. Although not visible the club face is perfectly square – in line with his left forearm.*

Look and Learn

(4) *Seve swings the club down powerfully on the inside. His right elbow is still quite close to his side and his weight is now transferring to his left side, the right heel already releasing from the ground as his hips turn through the shot.*

(5) *You can almost feel the power being released looking at this picture. Seve has great feel on his right side. You can see here how the right hand is beginning to turn over the left just after impact. The club face no longer faces the target.*

(6) *The power unleashed through the swing takes Seve to a full finish with his weight almost entirely on his left side. Like all the world's best players he swings in a controlled manner, only rarely finishing unbalanced.*

Bernhard Langer

Bernhard Langer, seen here, is practising short pitch shots which require good judgement of distance as well as pin-point accuracy, often enabling him to hole shots of this length, either to save par or to achieve a birdie. He has set up with slightly more weight on his left side, ball inside the left heel and has gripped down the shaft for extra control.

He has made the swing by using his arms rather than picking the club up with his hands. His wrists have cocked quite naturally in the backswing rather than being cocked too early, a fault of many higher handicappers. Because he has an open, yet narrow stance there is little weight transference.

Look and Learn

What a great picture to keep in mind! Note how firm his left wrist has remained at impact. He has allowed the loft of the club as it descends onto the ball to pitch it in the air; there is no attempt to scoop the ball up; it rises naturally if hit correctly.

The through swing is completed when his arms have reached about waist height, matching the length of the backswing. He has not allowed his right hand to rotate over the left but has held the blade square until well into the follow through, controlling the distance on this shot.

Look and Learn

Nick Faldo

(1) *Nobody in golf proves better than Nick Faldo that practice makes perfect. He has worked very hard to produce a compact swing. Watch his posture in this swing sequence, noting that the angle of his spine barely changes at all.*

(2) *The points we have highlighted earlier in this book are all evident here. Note especially that the leading edge of the club is square to the horizon.*

(3) *Compared to Payne Stewart (see pages 140-141) this looks only a three-quarter swing but Faldo is powerful enough to hit the ball a long way, even from a less than full backswing. His right arm is still quite close to his body and the spinal angle set at address has been retained.*

(4) *This position is one that most top class golfers achieve consistently. He is attacking the ball from inside the target line, his lower body leading the action. From here the club head is released into the ball.*

(5) *With his head still steady, eyes focussed on the ground, he swings through. Faldo worked long and hard to change his leg action from his earlier days and you can clearly see how his right heel has not released much from the ground at this point. The club face now points left of the target as it moves back inside the line.*

(6) *Now Faldo's right heel has released allowing him to swing through to a full finish. The spinal angle has still been maintained. As a player's height changes so must their posture – tall golfers, think carefully!*

Look and Learn

Payne Stewart

(1) *One of golf's more flamboyant characters, yet one of the nicest, has one of the most elegant swings in the game. His slim build produces one of the more fluent swings to be seen on the golf course. He starts, though, with an orthodox set up, the left arm and club shaft forming a straight line.*

(2) *Payne keeps his left arm extremely straight, almost stiff looking, though when his arms are horizontal his shoulders have already turned through 90 degrees. Compare his hip turn at this stage with that of Seve.*

(3) *At the top of the backswing his shoulders have turned more than 90 degrees, causing the shaft to be swung past the horizontal but, most importantly, still well under control. His hips have also turned more than the average yet the right leg is still providing good support. His head has turned slightly to the right, pulled round a little by the length of his turn on the backswing, yet he has not swayed at all.*

(4) *Halfway down, much of Payne's weight is on his left side. Note how the gap between his knees has widened compared to the last picture. You can see how he still has his wrists cocked ready to unleash the club head powerfully through the impact area.*

(5) *This point in the swing is almost the mirror image of picture 2. His hips and shoulders are turning through to face the target as the right hand and arm, having released their power, are turning over the left. His head has been kept in its original position but is rotating towards the target so that his swing is uninhibited.*

(6) *Payne's familiar, balanced finish with his body facing left of target, weight fully on his left side, hands high. This sequence clearly demonstrates that you can make a very full swing provided you maintain control and balance. If you overdo the swing you risk losing your balance. Turn fully on the backswing but maintain control.*

And Finally

Now that we have completed our lessons on golf technique the next thing to do is to get out and actually play golf.

Beginners should try to find easy courses – nine-hole par-3 courses if they exist in your area – as, naturally enough, it takes longer to get round a full-length course when you are still learning and it is impolite to hold up players behind you.

However, everyone has to start somewhere and no golfer would deny you the opportunity to improve your golf by playing on the course. Try, though, to avoid the busiest times such as weekend mornings when you might hold others up. When you do play try to avoid playing too slowly. Get to your ball as quickly as you can, remembering not to stand in front of any other player about to hit a shot. If you do have to look for a ball call the next group of golfers through straight away, rather than holding them up.

Most golf clubs have junior sections and, whilst many golf clubs have long waiting lists, most welcome junior members with hardly any waiting period.

Join a club close to you if you can; obviously if your parents or other friends belong to a club it makes sense to consider joining the same one – that way you'll have friends to play with.

Competitions are always stimulating and, once you overcome the inevitable nervousness about playing competitive golf, it should help you to improve.

Junior competitions are held regularly through the summer and, once you achieve a reasonable standard,

Take regular lessons from your golf professional.

And Finally

you could be selected to play in matches against other golf clubs in the area.

As you progress this could lead to your being chosen to play for the county or another local representative team. By this stage, though, your technique should have been further enhanced by additional lessons, including individual coaching from your club professional.

As an amateur golfer there are numerous opportunities for you to play in competitive matches, for your club, county or, eventually, country. Of course this takes time and extra devotion to the game. Very few golfers reach the top without extensive practice – most play or practise every day. For those dedicated enough the rewards can be great. Top amateurs play in international matches, the very best being selected for either the Walker Cup (men) or the Curtis Cup (ladies).

After that, or even before if your standard of golf is that good, a professional career beckons. What is important though, is that you continue to take lessons from a golf professional, to develop both your skills and mental ability. It has often been said that golf is a "mind" game; whilst that is true there is no substitute for continually striving to improve your technique.

The Golf Foundation

Finally, a brief word about the Golf Foundation. Founded in 1952 it is a national organisation dedicated to the promotion of junior golf in the UK. Its funding comes from golf equipment manufacturers and others associated with the game.

The Golf Foundation has available a comprehensive selection of videos and other material which are normally available to schools and other groups where a professional golfer can teach groups. It also operates several coaching schemes for younger golfers; those taking part can achieve merit awards as they progress. There is also a national competition for golfers under 15, in four age groups, based on a gross stroke-play format.

Players of the calibre of Peter Oosterhuis, Bernard Gallacher, Paul Way and Ronan Rafferty have all been helped by Golf Foundation schemes during their early years. Not all schools include golf in their sports curriculum – ask your school or your local golf club for details of the coaching schemes available from the Golf Foundation, 57 London Road, Enfield EN2 6DU.

And Finally

Daily Telegraph Junior Golfer of the Year

The Daily Telegraph
JUNIOR
GOLFER OF THE YEAR
COMPETITION

One of the best supported national competitions for young golfers is the Daily Telegraph Junior Golfer of the Year competition. Begun in the 1960s the event now attracts over 20,000 young golfers under eighteen years of age from clubs all over the British Isles.

Each golf club (and over 50% of all registered clubs in Britain participate) holds a preliminary event, played over eighteen holes of medal play, to find the club "champion" for this event, which is open to both boys and girls, there being two winners from each club, who each receive a winner's medal. There are runners-up prizes, too.

This part of the event runs at any time during the summer, and is held on your local course under the supervision of the club. The fifteen best scores for boys, and best four for girls, then receive an invitation to contest the final, normally held at the Penina course in Portugal in late autumn. The final is a medal play contest over 36 holes, the lowest gross score winning

1991 Girls Champion Mhairi McKay.

in both boys' and girls' categories. In the past few years the final has been televised.

In 1991 over 1600 clubs entered their local competition winners. The winners that year both came from Scotland (as they had in 1990), Mhairi McKay of Turnberry taking the girls' title with a 36 hole score of 146, Graham Davidson from Langholm in Dumfries & Galloway winning the boys' with 154, after a play-off.

1991 Boys Champion Graham Davidson.

Above: 1991 Club Competition Winner Kim Rostron (Clitheroe Golf Club), who just failed to qualify for the girl's final at Penina, but won her club competition beating the eight boy entrants.

And Finally

The Esso Junior Golf Classic

Another competition for young golfers is the Esso Junior Golf Classic, organised in conjunction with **Golf World** magazine. Unlike the Daily Telegraph competition, which is based on gross scores, the Esso Junior Golf Classic is a stableford competition, played with full handicaps (up to 36) open to golfers up to sixteen years of age.

Over 600 golf clubs organise their own qualifying contest, the winners going forward to twelve area finals, held throughout the country. From there the top twenty-four go forward to the Grand Final, held in 1991 at Walton Heath prior to the European Open. The final itself is played with a European Tour professional, a celebrity and two junior finalists playing together. Once again the result is decided on a best stableford score, with full handicap allowances.

The 1991 winner was fourteen-year old Perry Evans from Oxton, Nottinghamshire, who beat off the challenge of the other 7,000 entrants to win by two points. His handicap, which had been 24 when he qualified in May, had plummeted to 15 by the time he reached Walton Heath.

Pro Quote

Sandy Lyle

Sandy Lyle, although a Scot, grew up in Shropshire, not far from the Welsh border and the home of Ian Woosnam. Sandy was a prolific young golfer, coached by his father, himself a golf professional. By the time he was 17 he had won the Amateur Strokeplay Championship. Turning professional he won the Nigerian Open in his first year on the Safari Tour.

He went on to win the British Open in 1985 and the US Masters in 1988, beating his great contemporary rival, Nick Faldo, to both titles. He also won the Order of Merit in 1979, 1980 and 1985.

Although he went through a bare patch in 1989 and 1990, 1991 saw him back on the winning trail.

"With my young sons I teach them by just using about four clubs – a 5-wood, 6-iron, 8-iron and putter. Forget the rest. Until you become good at golf you don't need fourteen clubs in the bag. Just use three or four and learn to fashion shots with each club – become an artist with a golf club, so that you can do anything with it, rather than trying to use a different club for every shot.

"Also, you should make practising fun – learn to shape shots and make it interesting rather than just standing there hitting golf balls."

How To Become a Golf Professional

Golf is a wonderful game which millions of people worldwide play for pleasure. There are, as well, many thousands who have taken it up as their main profession, either as club professionals or tournament players.

In Britain the profession is run by the Professional Golfers' Association, the PGA, which imposes very high standards on those wishing to take up golf as a profession. The first stage towards becoming a professional is to become a PGA probationer, which allows a minimum period of six months at a club working under a fully qualified PGA member. During this period the probationer does not lose his or her amateur status. The idea of this scheme is to give the aspiring professional the opportunity to see if he or she really likes the idea of becoming a golf professional.

After a minimum six months working full time as a probationer, it is possible to apply to the PGA to become a registered trainee provided certain other criteria are satisfied. Apart from the six months' probationary experience, the PGA entrance examination in English and Maths must be passed (though a Grade A, B or C pass in GCSE or a Grade 1 in CSE in those subjects negates the need to take that entrance exam), and the applicant must have a registered handicap of 5 or less and be working full time with a qualified PGA professional.

A well-stocked 'high street' golf shop.

How To Become a Golf Professional

One question often asked is whether anyone with a higher handicap can enter the PGA as a trainee. The answer is, basically, no, although anyone entering the probationary period could, if they show promise, use this period to reduce their handicap under expert guidance.

Finding employment as a probationer is not always easy though the PGA does have an employment circular with situations available. It is possible to advertise in this at a very low rate. The address is given on page 158. Only those with a handicap of 6 or better can, however, advertise.

There is a YTS scheme in Britain run by Arrow Training, approved by the PGA, to help young people in their training during the probationary period. The address is also on page 158.

In other countries the conditions vary so an application should be made to the relevant authorities – any local club professional will be only too pleased to help with advice.

Trainees spend between three to four years learning the skills of a club professional which includes not only teaching golf but club repairs, shop and financial administration, rules of golf, public speaking and tournament organisation. Much of this training

Golf professionals spend much of their time teaching.

takes place with the PGA professional but there are also residential schools in the first and second years which the trainee must attend. These last for five days each and give the trainee the opportunity to cover all aspects of golf in both classroom and practical sessions.

Trainees must also play regularly in PGA-approved tournaments around the country, normally local or regional competitions where there is prize-money at stake. These days give the trainee the opportunity to get used to the preparation and attitude necessary to play competitive tournament golf. The trainee must play in at least twenty-five such events during the training period and must achieve a score which shows his playing ability to be within four strokes of scratch.

After the three years as a trainee the PGA Final Examination is taken, which again is residential and takes five days. Written, oral and practical examinations are held on the golf swing, teaching, merchandising, club repairs, rules of golf and tournament administration. All subjects must be passed. If any subjects are failed they may be re-taken. It is not necessary to re-take the subjects already passed.

The time limits surrounding trainee-ship are rigid, with no less than three years and no more than four years. If a trainee has failed in even one subject in the four-year period that, sadly, is the end of the road. There is no further opportunity, ever, to qualify as a PGA professional, though there is nothing to stop him or her continuing to work at a golf club as an assistant, but not in any teaching position.

Having passed all the examinations the trainee then applies to become a PGA member; the Executive Committee will ensure he or she has shown the personal qualities necessary to be accepted into the profession. Then comes the hard part!

With golf expanding there are many opportunities for employment as a golf professional at the numerous clubs and courses opening up throughout Britain and Europe. A period working as an assistant professional is highly recommended to gain more experience before becoming the head "pro" at a club. Almost every club professional has worked as an Assistant Professional for a few years to gain that extra experience so vital before taking on the full responsibilities of a club professional's position.

Club repairs are an essential part of a professional's skills.

How To Become a Golf Professional

Tournament Professionals

Some young men and women determine that they want to become tournament players rather than club professionals. The standards are extremely high and only the very best will ever make the grade, let alone become "stars".

Whilst the apparent riches of a tournament professional's life might appear tempting it is a very difficult profession to break into and only the very best will succeed in making a living, let alone becoming rich and famous.

Before even contemplating a professional life it is essential to have played amateur golf at the highest level, for county or country. The competition at this level is incredibly high, yet it starts at the local level with young golfers playing for their club in local or regional competitions before moving up to higher levels.

To become a touring professional takes enormous dedication and very advanced skills. About 700 young men – all of them playing off scratch or better – enter the annual pre-qualifying events for the European Tour. The top one hundred or so qualify for the European Tour Winter School, held at present in southern France each November.

Over six days at the Winter School the young hopefuls receive expert tuition and play against each other under tournament conditions. Only the top forty will gain their "card" enabling them to play for one season on the European Tour. Past winners of the Tour School include Sandy Lyle, Gordon Brand Jnr and José Maria Olazabal. The standard is that high.

At the end of the season the top 120 golfers on the European Tour (together with those in the exempt categories such as Faldo, Woosnam and other champions) will automatically be of-

Despite Sam Torrance's smile it's not all easy going being a tournament golfer.

fered a "card" for the following season – all others will have to qualify again at the Winter School to prove they are good enough to compete at the highest level of golf.

For those who are not quite good enough to gain their full card there is a secondary tour – the Challenge Tour – which plays events all over Europe. The top ten money-winners on this tour automatically qualify for their full European card for the following season.

It is, as a touring professional, anything but an easy life. Only the relatively few who make it to the top of the profession live in anything like luxury. For the remainder the season comprises a lot of hard travel from tournament to tournament, constantly living out of a suitcase, and practising almost every waking minute, week in, week out.

With tournaments most weeks of the season in Europe, the professionals arrive on a Monday at whatever event they are playing, have a practice round on Tuesday to familiarise themselves with the course, and then spend the Wednesday probably practising on a nearby course whilst a select few play in the traditional pro-am match which is now the curtain raiser to every major tournament.

Thursday and Friday are tournament days, very often with an early start. Many tournaments begin at 7.15am so with half an hour's practice beforehand the professional needs to be at the course around 6am – a very early start from the nearby hotel or guest house.

The "cut" is made on Friday night with the top players going through to

A golf professional's life is one long round of tournaments.

How To Become a Golf Professional

compete in the last two rounds on Saturday and Sunday. The others either go home or go on to the next week's destination to get in some extra practice. For those not making the cut there is no pay! Hotel, travel and caddies' bills still need paying, though.

Every professional needs to get into the top ten or twenty at least a couple of times a year to make it worthwhile, otherwise the drain on the finances can be pretty drastic. Although many professionals manage to find a sponsor to help them in their early years on tour, that sponsorship may end unless the results are satisfactory.

Even top professionals like Bernhard Langer are continually perfecting their game and are ready to seek sound advice.

How To Become a Golf Professional

Club Professionals

Of course, once a young professional has tried the touring life he or she may decide that life as a club professional is more suitable – it will certainly be less problematical! Others decide right away, after qualifying, that they wish to become a club pro.

To start with some time spent as an assistant professional is a very good idea, learning the best way to run a golf shop and look after club members.

There are many opportunities to become an assistant professional, and it is advisable to work at a couple of golf clubs, under the guidance of experienced professionals, before deciding to apply for a "head" professional's position.

Taking over a club shop entails buying the stock of golf equipment and clothes, often financed by loans which need to be repaid at some time. Members will require lessons and it is expected that the professional is available to play golf with members from time to time.

The life of a club professional is anything but nine-to-five. Most club shops are open from 8am or earlier to around 8pm in the evening, possibly later in mid-summer, much earlier in the dark days of winter. Saturdays and Sundays are always busy days, throughout the year, so the club professional will not have weekends off, nor many days in the week – one-and-a-half days off a week is average.

As well as teaching, there are always club repairs to be handled,

A club professional has a very busy shop to look after as well as giving lessons.

questions about rules to be answered; and all the time a shop full of equipment and clothes needs to be maintained, for sales of goods are a vital part of a professional's livelihood. Assistants also have to be employed, for no golf professional can run a club and shop alone.

It is not an easy life, yet it is, for those dedicated enough, very enjoyable and satisfying with realistic financial rewards. What most club professionals regard as the biggest reward, though, is seeing people they teach improve and enjoy their golf even more.

Sales of golf equipment – such as shoes – help to provide an income for the club professional.

Green fees paid, sales completed. Golfers at this busy club get on with playing golf.

Glossary

Ace	A hole in one.
Address	The position taken by a player when he is preparing to swing.
Air Shot	Hitting at but failing to make contact with the ball.
Albatross	A score of three under the par for the hole (eg 2 on a par 5).
Apron	The fringe of the green, mown shorter than the fairway but not as short as the green itself. Also referred to as the fringe.
Birdie	A score of one under par (eg 3 on a par 4).
Bogey	A score of one over par (eg 5 on a par 4).
Borrow	The amount of deviation from a straight line you need to strike a putt on a sloping green.
Boundary	The outside perimeter of the golf course, which is out of bounds.
Bunker	A hollow in the ground normally filled with sand. If it is not filled with sand (as can happen with grass bunkers) it does not count as a hazard. You can not ground your club in a hazard.
Carry	The distance a ball travels in the air before it hits the ground. You often need to know the 'carry' to get over a bunker or stream, for example.
Casual Water	Temporary water on the course which is not part of the normal design of the course. You are allowed to lift the ball from casual water and play it from a dry spot on the course without penalty. Ice and snow can be either casual water or a loose impediment. Dew is not casual water and you have to play the ball as it lies.
Chip	A low, running shot to the green.
Choke down	Gripping the club further down the handle to give better control or to decrease the distance the club will hit.
Closed face	When the blade of the club is turned left of target.
Closed stance	When the body and feet line are pointing right of the target.
Cocking the wrists	The bending of the wrists as you swing the club back.
Cut	A shot which is faded, starting straight but turning right. In professional golf tournaments there is also a 'cut' halfway through, when those golfers above a certain score are eliminated.

Glossary

Divot	A piece of turf which is removed from the ground by the club when you hit a shot. It should always be replaced except on the tee.
Dog-Leg	A fairway which turns either left or right, normally at the driving distance.
Dormy	A situation in matchplay when one player is leading by the same number of holes as there are left to play.
Draw	A shot which starts straight but turns gently left as it progresses.
Drop	A player drops a ball when the original has gone out of bounds, is unplayable or is lost. In both cases penalty strokes are added.There are also free drops (without penalty) if the ball is in a 'Ground Under Repair' area, is in casual water or is impeded by an immovable obstruction.
Eagle	A score of two under par (eg 3 on a par 5).
Fore	What you must shout if your ball is flying dangerously toward someone else.
Gimme	A putt left close enough to the hole for the next to be conceded by your opponent in matchplay only, though you do count the putt you would have needed to sink it.
Ground Under Repair	An area of the golf course which is being repaired and which you are normally forbidden to play from, receiving a free drop. Often marked with white lines on the ground with the letters 'GUR'.
Honour	Apart from on the first tee the player with the honour is the one who won the last hole (matchplay) or had the lower score on it (strokeplay).
Hood	To turn the club face over more by pressing forward on the club – this makes the ball fly lower.
Hook	An uncontrolled shot which flies left. A draw is controlled.
Hosel	The base of the club shaft where it joins the blade.
Links	A seaside golf course – the ball runs further on the hard turf.
Local Rules	Each course has its own local rules which contain important rulings on several aspects of the course. They must be read before you commence play.
Loft	The angle of the slope on the club face (see page 12).
Mulligan	If a player hits a terrible first shot he is often allowed a 'mulligan' by his colleagues in a friendly game. It is, though, totally illegal.

Glossary

Provisional Ball   If a player has seen a shot disappear into an area of trees, deep rough or near a hazard, a provisional ball is often played from the same spot. If the first ball cannot be found, the provisional is played, adding a penalty stroke.

Scratch   A handicap of zero.

Shank   A shot hit off the hosel of the club.

Slice   An uncontrolled shot hit to the right.

SSS   Standard Scratch Score, the gauge for handicaps. It may vary from the par for a course, as it is based on the difficulty of the course, not just the length.

Stableford   A game in which players get one point for a bogey, two for a par, three for a birdie and so on.

Stroke Index   A measure of the relative difficulty of each hole, the easiest being index 18, the hardest being index 1.

Yips   Caused by nerves when putting, making it difficult to hold the putter steady.

Useful Addresses

Esso Junior Golf Classic
Tournament Controller,
Esso Junior Golf Classic
Golf World
37 Millharbour,
Isle of Dogs,
London E14 9TX

Daily Telegraph
Junior Golfer of the Year
PO Box 9
Southsea PO4 0BR

The Golf Foundation
57 London Road
Enfield EN2 6DU

PGA,
Apollo House,
The Belfry,
Sutton Coldfield,
B76 9PR

Arrow Training Services,
12 Welsh Street,
Chepstow,
NP6 5NL

Index

page

Address   20-26
Aiming   see "Target, lining up to"
Alignment   5, 23
Arc, of swing   41
Backswing   29, 31, 33, 34, 35
Bad lies   76-81
Ball position   22
Bunkers (see also "bunker shots")   9
Bunker shots   23, 69-74, 96, 107
Casting (of the club)   36, 45
Casual water   99, 100
Chipping   64, 65, 125
Cross slope lies   120
Cocking (of wrists)   34, 37, 81
Divot   60
Downhill lies   119
Drop (free or penalty) 94, 98, 99, 102
Equipment   12, 13
Forearms, strengthening   125
Gloves, golf   14
Graphite, shafts, care of   13
Grip, taking of   15
Grip, baseball   16, 17
Grip, interlocking   16, 17
Grip, strong   18
Grip, Vardon   16, 17
Grip, weak   18
Ground Under Repair   97, 100
Handicap system   10-11
Hole-in-one   11
Hook   40, 55
Hosel   12
Immovable obstructions   97
Insert, of club   12
Leading edge, of club   12

page

Lie, of club   13
Loose impediments   95
Loose impediments in bunker   96
Movable obstructions   95
Out of bounds   97
PGA   148-150
Par, description of   10, 109
Pitch shot   23, 64, 66, 125
Pivot   32
Plane, of swing   41
Posture   26, 27
Pre-shot routine   21
Putters   13, 83
Putting   64, 83-91, 111
Rough   10, 77-81
Shank, part of club   12
Shoes   14
Slice   40, 55
Staked trees   94
Stance, width of   22, 51, 60, 66, 85
Stones, in bunkers   96
Stroke index   11, 109
Target, lining up to   21, 88
Tee shot   22, 51, 93
Toe, of club   12
Trees, staked   94
Uphill lies   119
"V"s of thumb and forefinger   16
Weight distribution 23, 34, 36, 38, 51,
                                71, 73, 79, 85
Weight transference   37, 38
Whipping, of club   12
Wind, playing in   112-115
Wood, playing from fairway   22, 59
Wrists, strengthening of   125

No matter how good you become you will always benefit from expert tuition and guidance – and hours of practice.